IN PURSUIT

David Reichenbaugh *with Lori Widmer*

ForeEdge

THE HUNT FOR THE BELTWAY SNIPERS

ForeEdge

An imprint of University Press of New England

www.upne.com

© 2018 David Charles Reichenbaugh

All rights reserved

Manufactured in the United States of America

Designed by Mindy Basinger Hill

Typeset in Minion Pro

Library of Congress Cataloging-in-Publication Data

Names: Reichenbaugh, David, author. | Widmer, Lori, author.

Title: In pursuit : the hunt for the Beltway snipers / David Reichenbaugh,
with Lori Widmer.

Description: Lebanon, NH : ForeEdge, [2018] | Includes bibliographical
references and index.

Identifiers: LCCN 2018023846 (print) | LCCN 2018025440 (ebook) |
ISBN 9781512603262 (epub, pdf, & mobi) | ISBN 9781512603255 (pbk.)

Subjects: LCSH: Muhammad, John Allen, 1960–2009. | Malvo, Lee Boyd,
1985– | Serial murders—Washington Metropolitan Area—Case studies. |
Criminal snipers—Washington Metropolitan Area—Case studies. | Serial
murder investigation—Washington Suburban Area—Case studies.

Classification: LCC HV6534.W3 (ebook) | LCC HV6534.W3 R45 2018 (print) |
DDC 364.152/320975—dc23

LC record available at https://lccn.loc.gov/2018023846

5   4   3   2   1

The greater the loyalty of a group toward the group,
the greater is the motivation among the members to achieve
the goals of the group, and the greater the probability
that the group will achieve its goals.

Rensis Likert

CONTENTS

IN PURSUIT

PROLOGUE

Tuesday, October 22, 2002. We now knew their names. After three weeks, ten killings, and four injuries, more than a dozen of us were sitting in our makeshift command center looking at the faces of the two people who had done so much killing.

In front of me on the computer screen was a photo of Lee Malvo. Christ, he was just a kid—seventeen years old. A Jamaican immigrant kid. Could this really be a mastermind of one of the worst shooting rampages this country had ever seen? Could this kid really have pulled the trigger on so many people?

He and his mentor, John Allen Muhammad, had terrorized the Beltway area of Washington, D.C., Maryland, and Virginia in one of the most bizarre crime sprees ever—targeting random people, shooting to kill, and holding the tristate area hostage for twenty days now. For eighteen of those days, we at the Sniper Murder Task Force (SNIPMUR) had pored over thousands of tips, phone calls, and minimal evidence trying to track down one thing, *anything*, that would help us identify the perpetrators. Now we had names.

For three weeks, federal, state, and local law enforcement agencies had been working together to stop the rampage. We were exhausted; we had been at it around the clock, taking breaks only when ordered to, and chasing dead ends for way too long. We had searched in vain for a white van, which witnesses claimed to have seen at several of the crime scenes. And time wasn't on our side—the victim totals were rising, and every day that these killers stayed on the streets meant more victims.

Not that there were many people still on the streets. Through-out the area, residents were in hiding. They hid behind their cars while pumping gas. Restaurants' shades were drawn, and their parking lots were nearly empty. Grocery stores, shops, and other-wise busy streets looked abandoned. Schools were in lockdown during school hours, and heavily armed troopers, officers, and SWAT teams patrolled the perimeters. Playgrounds were empty, activities were canceled. Life had come to a standstill as residents held their collective breath.

But now we had names. With those names, the details were fall-ing into place. No more white van; the vehicle was now identified as a blue Chevrolet Caprice. Inside the joint operations center for SNIPMUR, the excitement was palpable.

As Tuesday turned into Wednesday, I was ordered to go home and get some sleep. I left the joint operations center—the JOC, as we called it—and headed home after 1 a.m. Then back to the JOC by 5:30 a.m. Once again, I spent most of the day with the team re-viewing what we knew and strategizing our next moves. Little did we know that our luck was about to change. At 10:30 that night, I was sent home to rest. Then my police radio crackled and came alive. It was Sergeant Bob Hundertmark.

"Car 662, we just received a cell phone call from a citizen in the westbound rest area on I-70. The caller advised that there is a Caprice in the rest area parking lot, and then repeated the tag that we had put out over the air."

They say that fighter pilots train for years honing a combat skill set that they may never get a chance to use—and if they do, it may all be over in less than a minute. I was about to put to the test every skill I had learned in my twenty-two-year career as a law enforcement officer: courage, tenacity, control, command. Everything I did, everything my team was about to do, had to be executed with precision. Failure meant troopers could die and more residents would be at risk.

We couldn't fail. We had no choice.

1

On September 11, 2001, law enforcement changed—again. On that catastrophic day, I was serving as the detective sergeant at the Maryland State Police's Frederick Barrack, which is located near Catoctin Mountain approximately forty miles north of Washington, D.C., straight up Interstate 270. This is close to the site of Camp David, the presidential retreat, which is on top of the mountain. Beneath it is another semisecret government facility, officially named "Site R." Insiders call it "the underground Pentagon."

We stood in the radio room watching TV news reports, dumbfounded by what we were seeing. I called my wife, who was working the emergency room at Frederick Memorial Hospital, to see if the kids had gone to school that day. "We're under attack," I said. "Are you seeing the same thing I am?" I told her I didn't know when I would be home. We quickly threw together a loose plan to take care of our family.

Suddenly, the red phone rang. Everyone stopped moving and stared at it. The red light blinked incessantly. This phone rang every Friday at 3 p.m., a test. Never any day but Friday. Today was a Tuesday. The phone, a direct line between our barrack and Camp David, was to ring *only* in the event that the president's retreat was under attack or in danger of being attacked.

Camp David was protected by well-armed, highly trained

Marines. Our role, once that phone rang, was to provide cannon fodder by manning the outer perimeter or checkpoints. I don't recall who answered that day, but the orders came down: Site R was being fully activated, and our federal government was being moved to various locations. Also, there was talk that much of the population of the District of Columbia was preparing to flee Washington. We were about to receive something like a half-million people running north right into our laps.

There is nothing like the realization that your planning and practice, or lack thereof, is about to bite you in the ass when the real crisis starts. Someone grabbed a three-ring binder from a shelf in the communications room. Inside that binder were detailed plans outlining our entire response effort from that minute forward. These plans had been discussed—every once in a while—but the truth is, we were ill prepared, understaffed, and would quickly become overwhelmed. So we did what we always do in dicey moments—reverted to our long-held, unofficial state police motto: "One riot, one trooper—put your Stetson on." In other words, never show the public that you're scared or unsure. Stand tall and get the job done.

In the days and weeks following September 11, we learned that one of the hijackers who flew planes into the World Trade Center had been stopped the night before the attacks by a uniformed Maryland state trooper on I-95 north of Baltimore. Suspecting that something was wrong, the trooper conducted every criminal record check he had access to, but found nothing. So he issued a citation, and the man continued on his way. Had the trooper had access to the FBI watch list, or to any other intelligence databases, he might have been able to detain the man, throw off the timing of the plan, maybe even stop the attacks. We also learned that several of the terrorists had spent time residing in the Laurel,

Maryland, area, a fifteen- to twenty-minute drive from our Intelligence Division offices. In other words, the terrorists pulled this off right under our noses, and we never had a clue until it was too late.

But, of course, in the days pre-9/11 none of us would have been expecting anything like what happened—just as we didn't anticipate the anthrax attacks that began a mere one week later. The FBI was quick to narrow down the source of the anthrax—it was used at the chemical and biological warfare labs at Fort Detrick in Frederick County. But the investigation came too late for five people who were killed by the substance, and for seventeen others who were infected. Once again, we in the Maryland State Police—the MSP—were painfully aware that an evil plan had been formulated and hatched in our state.

The entire country now had a very bad case of the jitters. We in Maryland, which is full of high-value targets, were on edge, now *expecting* another attack but not knowing where, when, or how. Governor Parris Glendening and the MSP's Colonel David Mitchell put the State Police Criminal Intelligence Division back in the game, hoping to stave off future attacks. This was a welcome move, but how long would it last? Law enforcement in the United States, particularly at the local, city, and state level, is cyclical in nature—and when pressed, it tends to be reactive.

Like most such agencies, the Maryland State Police has always been hampered by tight budgets and limited resources, even though the workload always seems to expand. Doing more with the same or fewer resources is normal. When I started my career in the early '80s, every barrack had a crime prevention program, and there was at least one supervisor and one trooper assigned to work on crime prevention programs in the community. However, as the job changed because of some evident need—or oftentimes as a knee-jerk reaction to some new thing that happened—manpower had to be reallocated, and forward-thinking, proactive programs were sacrificed. Troopers within those programs were reassigned, and the programs were soon forgotten.

Such was the case with the Criminal Intelligence Division. In the early 1980s, when First Lady Nancy Reagan declared a war on drugs, the state police were called on to go in the direction the federal government wanted law enforcement to take. With the federal funds we received, the MSP was able to add a few additional troopers—but nowhere near the number needed to staff a newly formed Narcotics Division. One of the casualties of this situation was the Intelligence Division, whose ranks were raided to staff Narcotics. The Intelligence Division was reduced to civilian employees and a couple of troopers and wound up accepting every odds-and-ends job that didn't fit into any other division's job description. Intelligence's new duties consisted of gathering and tracking race-related traffic stop and search statistics to satisfy court-ordered consent decrees, and tracking how many crimes, as outlined by the Uniform Crime Reporting system, were occurring in each of Maryland's twenty-three counties. The state police were ordered to collect a mass of statistics but weren't provided with the help needed to complete the task. In other words, the Intelligence Division was reduced to recordkeeping and statistics. It had become an effective intelligence-gathering unit in name only.

Now, immediately following 9/11, I was promoted from detective sergeant to lieutenant and transferred to the reborn Criminal Intelligence Division. My orders were simple: look at the ranks and choose troopers with the needed skill set, then get boots on the ground gathering intelligence. In that, I was to coordinate with allied state agencies and the feds to make sure there were no more surprises. I was charged with training the troopers on covert operations and teaching them to track and infiltrate groups that could be a threat to national or state security.

For many years we had known that money garnered from criminal enterprises in the United States was being funneled back to terrorist states to be used against us. So part of our new process involved locating and tracking the movements of drug dealers, organized crime, and organized theft rings that were operating within the state. Within a few short months, we had seen the word "terrorist" become a regular part of the vernacular. All of us knew our focus had changed, and these challenges were ones we had to learn to prevent and respond to—and fast.

2

October 2, 2002. The one-year anniversary of the 9/11 attacks had come and gone. The Maryland State Police had established undercover operators who were beginning to infiltrate groups that we had identified as suspect, or that were known to include people on the terrorist watch list. With the aid of troopers and commanders from all twenty-three barracks, the Criminal Intelligence Division had identified hundreds of potential targets as well as critical infrastructure, and was attempting to harden those targets by working not only with the federal government, but also with our citizens and private industry.

In addition to military installations and high-value terrorist targets, critical infrastructure included bridges, stadiums, communications hubs, and other public and private structures that, if attacked, could cause a serious disruption of life. We had also identified locations and facilities where multiple casualties could occur during an attack, and had developed plans for making those much more difficult to breach. We had also worked with local, county, and city first-responders statewide to update old, out-of-date plans on what to do if something did happen.

After identifying every critical business and infrastructure in the state, we initiated ongoing outreach programs to make those businesses and infrastructure managers aware of the latest intelligence that we could share with them, and we encouraged them to take steps to protect themselves against a potential attack. It was sort of the old crime prevention program on steroids. We helped them identify weaknesses in their physical security and familiarized ourselves with what each company did in order to evaluate what, if any, value it would have to a terrorist trying to disrupt business or damage our country in any way. It was shocking how many facilities there were in Maryland that, if attacked, could affect not just Maryland, but the entire nation as well.

Obviously, companies with U.S. government contracts—especially those related to the defense industry—were considered high on the list of potential targets. We encouraged those companies to report anything suspicious to us, no matter how insignificant it may seem. We provided them with information on how to spot persons or groups that may be watching their businesses. In private industry, these precautions would have been called a "continuity of business plan"; in our world, they were emergency response plans. Once again the state police didn't receive additional troopers or resources; we were just spreading the peanut butter a little thinner on the bread.

Then, on the evening of October 2, a bullet pierced a glass storefront window at a Michaels craft store at Northgate Plaza in Aspen Hill, Montgomery County. The incident was treated as a random shooting. No one was hurt—the bullet went through the storefront window, missing the cashier working at her register.

Because of our heightened focus on terrorism, this shooting nearly went unnoticed.

Until it happened again that same day. Shortly after the first shooting, James Martin was loading groceries into the back of his car at a Shoppers Food Warehouse parking lot on Georgia Avenue in Wheaton when a bullet killed him on the spot.

Not knowing the reasons for either shooting, law enforcement considered Martin's murder a random act of violence committed by an unknown person. Any number of reasons could have applied: robbery, revenge, jealousy, another gang-related killing. The Montgomery County police began their homicide investigation into the Martin murder just as they would for any other homicide in their area. As of yet, no one had any reason to tie the two shootings together.

Montgomery County is a heavily populated urban county north of Washington, D.C. Most of the county is located outside the Washington Beltway. The county shares borders with Prince Georges County to the south and east, Howard County to northeast, and Frederick County to the north, with the state of Virginia across the Potomac River to the west. Montgomery County is home to a mixed bag of residents, from the very wealthy to the working class. It serves as headquarters for many different high-tech companies, most of which do business with the federal government.

When the first bullet pierced the window at the Michaels store, police assumed it was either random violence or the careless act of some drunk or vandal bent on tearing up somebody else's property just for the hell of it. In a county the size of Montgomery—approximately nine hundred thousand people—police received dozens of destruction-of-property calls every day. In the northern, more rural part of the county, it's not unusual to come across road signs with a bullet hole or two punched through them. No one at either Michaels or the Montgomery County Police Department could have predicted the horror show that was about to befall their community—in fact, the entire region.

3

October 3 started uneventfully, just another day. Like always, I made my hour-long commute to the Intelligence Division offices in a nondescript office complex in Columbia, near Baltimore. Our offices were unmarked except for the name "ND Incorporated" in small lettering on the building. That was to keep the average bad guy from knowing what was inside. In a neighboring building, just around the corner, the Narcotics Division had its offices.

My car was a full-size Caprice—obviously an unmarked police car: cop wheels, cop tires, no shiny extras like you see on an automobile the average civilian would drive. My car also had several obvious antennas on the trunk that made it either a police car or a tuna boat. By Maryland State Police standards, it was one of our newer cars—only 150,000 miles on it. The car's numbered identifier was 662—the 600 series indicating vehicles assigned to Intel.

I arrived at the office well before 8 a.m. and spent the early part of the morning going over intelligence reports from the day before. I also reviewed written reports from troopers in the field so I would be familiar with every active investigation. One of my jobs was to make sure we stayed focused on terrorism prevention, and to guide and direct troopers tasked with infiltrating or gathering intel on groups we were concerned with. We had a staff of more than twenty talented civilian analysts. Their role was to make contact every day with colleagues around the state and with federal agencies to keep apprised of the latest concerns on the home front. The analysts tracked and made sense of reports and open-source intelligence that flowed across the news channels, newspapers, and the Web.

Those of us in law enforcement were very much on edge. We no longer thought in terms of "if" another terrorist attack would happen. Now it was "when." We had troopers in the field. Our daily communications with allied agencies in Maryland, Pennsylvania, Virginia, and the District of Columbia, as well as with a number of federal agencies, produced reams of data. It was my job to review this data and, along with Detective Sergeant Dan Cornwell and Captain A. J. McAndrew, make sound recommendations to state police leadership on how to prevent the next attack. We spent every single day looking for that needle in a haystack, in a field full of haystacks.

Captain McAndrew was at the state police headquarters in Pikesville that morning, conducting what had become a daily intelligence briefing to Colonel David Mitchell and senior MSP leadership. Sometime around 10 a.m. my phone rang. It was Major Jimmy Ballard, the regional commander for the Metro region. Major Ballard also served as the commander of STATE—the state police version of a SWAT team.

Major Ballard said that Montgomery County law enforcement was responding to "a series of shootings." He didn't know who, or when, or how many; the only information he had was that it appeared to be the work of a sniper or snipers, and that they may be in a white van. He said that Montgomery County police were overwhelmed and were requesting assistance from the state police. We decided we would make the Rockville Barrack a temporary command center. All Maryland State Police resources would be directed there, pending further assignment.

After hanging up, I directed troopers to respond immediately to Rockville. Then I called Captain McAndrew, who said he would brief the colonel on the situation. With everyone notified, I began preparing myself to leave. There was a jumble of things running through my mind. I had snippets of information on what was happening, but everything was in that initial stage of confusion that occurs during every crisis, no matter how well trained or prepared you are. I quickly scanned the stack of intelligence that was still waiting for my review, making sure I hadn't missed anything. As I headed for the door, I tapped two civilian analysts to take with me. We would definitely need them. Who knew what this was—some sort of terrorist attack designed to create panic? If so, it appeared to be working. The public was already skittish; if they got wind of this, that panic was going to reach epidemic proportions within a few hours.

4

At times of crisis, we cops fall back on our years of training, the learning that over time has become second nature to the professionals we have become. Before I was ten years old I knew I wanted to be a trooper. I had grown up in rural western Pennsylvania in a small village called Spring Church. It was rare that we would see police at all, but occasionally I would spot a Pennsylvania state trooper ride past the house.

I was in awe of the troopers, with their highly pressed uniforms, their breeches flared at the sides and tucked into polished black boots. They wore their flat-brim hats tilted forward over their eyes, the strap hitting their chins just beneath their lips. Then there was the gun: huge Smith & Wesson revolvers hung in holsters on their belts. To a young boy, they looked like cannons. And the troopers themselves seemed to be ten feet tall.

The few troopers I had met rarely smiled, but they were always kind and friendly at the same time. To a third grader at Sunnyside Elementary School, they were the good guys—the heroes. Who wouldn't want to be a trooper? I pretty much made up my mind then that I was going to be a trooper, even if I had to go to Alaska to do it.

After graduating from Indiana University of Pennsylvania in December 1981, I was accepted into the Maryland State Police Academy and started my training in Pikesville, Maryland, in July 1982. At that time, the MSP still had a very robust, forward-looking Criminal Intelligence Division consisting of sworn troopers and civilian analysts. They tracked all kinds of groups, from organized crime to the Ku Klux Klan to motorcycle gangs.

In December of 1982 I graduated from the Maryland State Police Academy, fulfilling a lifelong dream. But there was little time to celebrate my finally becoming a trooper; I was sent immediately to Calvert County to work in uniform at the Prince Frederick Barrack. Prince Frederick was a full-service MSP barrack. And because the Calvert County sheriff's department was so small (their officers went home at midnight), we also served as the police for the county.

The Prince Frederick Barrack was a great place to learn to be a cop, but living in Calvert County sucked if you were a young, single trooper. About the only things there in those days were the Patuxent Naval Air Station and the Calvert Cliffs Nuclear Power Plant. There were no movie theaters, and only one shopping center—at least it included a grocery store, a gym, and a couple of other stores. There was one McDonald's and three High's Dairy stores that closed at midnight. When you worked night patrol at Prince Frederick, you made sure you were on the road early enough to get to one of the High's stores before it closed. Otherwise, it was a long night without coffee, sodas, or snacks.

My living arrangements did little to improve the dating scene. I was taken in by two senior troopers—Vonzell Ward and Joe Pruitt—who occupied a very large house all by themselves. The price was right—free. In fact, it was free for all of us. It was common in those days for absentee landowners in Calvert County to get troopers to live on their properties rent free in exchange for the comfort of knowing that there was a marked state police car, otherwise known as a "roller," parked out front. The three of us lived in a modern, two-story, five-bedroom home that had been built on the foundation of a turn-of-the-century manor.

Vonzell and Joe were great roommates, but also great tutors. They taught me about respect for the community, respect for the job, respect for other troopers. From these guys I learned that the MSP was a family. Every trooper, on the road or otherwise, would be there for me if needed. And I was expected to be there for them in return—an obligation that continued even through a trooper's death. The Death Relief Fund was a sacred part of being a Maryland state trooper. Every time a current or retired trooper died, every other trooper would contribute five dollars to the fund. This was a way for the surviving family to immediately receive cash to deal with all the things that go along with death of a loved one.

The Death Relief Fund was simple in the abstract, but more complicated in day-to-day troopering. Upon completing my field training, I had to make one last check ride with my corporal before I was cut loose. Corporal Dave Cameron was not one to suffer fools. After spending about six hours driving him around, making traffic stops, and handling every call for service that came over the radio, I had just completed a traffic stop. When I got back in the car, Corporal Cameron didn't look happy. He stared at me for what seemed an eternity. "Give me five dollars," he finally said.

"Sir?"

"Give me five goddamn dollars right now. I want a refund."

Confused, I stared back. I didn't know what to say.

"If you keep making traffic stops the way you're doing them, you're gonna get killed. I don't want to have to pay five dollars because you're fucking stupid, Boot."

I reached for my wallet and produced the five dollars. I had only about eight dollars to my name at the time, but there was no way in hell I was going to refuse. Cameron snatched the bill out of my hand and shoved it in his pocket. "We ask for troopers," he muttered, "and they send us dumb fucking kids who'll get themselves killed before the shine is off their damn boots."

At the academy we were taught how to safely make a traffic stop, which entailed watching the people in the stopped car while keeping an eye on the traffic coming up behind you. It was no secret that some people got a kick out of swerving close enough to the trooper to knock the Stetson off his or her head, and of course there were drunk drivers who were attracted to the police lights and would drive off the road and smack into the police car.

What they didn't teach us was how to do all these things if we were left-handed. Corporal Cameron was left-handed, same as me, and he had to learn this *outside* the academy. That day he passed those lessons on to me. They involved parking at an offset angle to protect myself—and the other driver—from oncoming traffic; that angle also gave me a place behind the engine block to take cover if the stopped driver decided to pull a weapon on me. Finally, I learned to sidle up to the stopped car with my right side to the driver's window—and then to turn and position myself by his rearview mirror, with my gun side toward his car.

These were lessons I never forgot, and they probably saved my life more times than I realize. Also, Corporal Cameron helped me understand the fine balance between doing the job with respect for others while never forgetting that at *any* time someone might try to kill me. The job was dangerous, a sobering lesson. Yet despite that, it was a job that fit me perfectly.

5

Within six months of my time at Prince Frederick, I had learned how much I enjoyed criminal investigation and solving crimes, even the seemingly trivial ones. It was always easy for me to talk to people and gain their trust.

I also learned that one of the most important things in the state police was how well you played softball.

Being a little lonely at Prince Frederick, I had requested a transfer to the similar sounding but totally different Frederick Barrack, in Frederick County, less than an hour's drive from where my brother lived in West Virginia. Frederick was also a full-service barrack, meaning I would be exposed to much more in the way of criminal investigation. When I made the request, I was told that the waiting list would be long—it seemed that *everyone* wanted to be assigned to Frederick.

But timing is everything. To my surprise, my request was granted quickly because, apparently, the Frederick Barrack softball team needed a replacement outfielder, and I had played a lot of baseball as a kid. My transfer came through two weeks before the annual state police softball tournament, the annual brawl for the honor of holding the trophy as state police champion for the next year. My fellow troopers at Prince Frederick weren't very happy with me, but all I could do was salute, say "yes sir," and hustle to Frederick in time for my first assigned shift. I soon found myself standing in right-center field, my schedule magically arranged so that I had three days off in a row—the same three days the tournament was being played. New troopers fresh out of the academy *never* get three days off in a row. My new team went on to win the tournament that year. Prince Frederick Barrack took third behind Waterloo Barrack. My old teammates found consolation in calling me all sorts of names, but it was all in fun.

I enjoyed my uniform service at Frederick Barrack. I felt at home there. And for the rest of my career, I would find myself coming back to this place that had done so much to shape me. For the first couple of years, I dedicated myself to learning. The more I focused on criminal investigation, the more I realized I had found my calling. I did fine with the traffic side of the job, but I never set the world on fire when it came to writing traffic citations. I came to be known as "Trooper Black Cloud" because I had a habit of showing up in exactly the right place when a robbery, assault, or some other serious act was happening. It was a little freaky, I admit: several times I had stopped in the middle of the night to check on a random business only to discover it was in the process of getting burglarized. I was falling into great arrests. One of my sergeants told me I was either a very lucky trooper or constantly on the hunt for trouble. He said something else that stuck with me: "If you're not more careful, you're going to get killed."

Frederick County in the mid-1980s was going through a rough transition. With crack cocaine becoming more rampant in America, that and other drugs were finding their way into our rural county. Like many states during that era, Maryland was playing catch-up. We had just four or five state police narcotics agents for the entire state. Looking to increase those numbers, the Frederick Barrack commander recruited me to start working undercover out of our barrack.

I was thrilled. Here was my opportunity to get out of uniform and earn my way onto the staff of the Frederick Barrack Criminal Investigation Section. But when I was pulled off road detail, I had zero experience in undercover work. I thought the job was to go buy drugs from people and then arrest them.

My first assignment was to spend a few weeks working out of the Waterloo Barrack in what was then known as the "Special Services" section. Thinking I would impress them on my first day, I showed up at Waterloo looking the way I thought a drug dealer should look: blue jeans, a T-shirt, an Orioles cap, and driving a beat-up old Mustang that had been seized by the MSP. Little did I know how much I stood out. I also didn't know that I was about to meet a legend.

Detective Sergeant Warren Rineker, known far and wide as Rinky, sat in his office reviewing reports while I stood at attention in front of his desk. He didn't even look up for the longest time. Of course I had heard about him, and from all the stories I had figured he would stand ten feet tall and have bulging muscles. But the guy I was staring at might have hit five-foot-eight at most, and he was definitely on the pudgy side. He sported a full beard and long hair—blond and graying—that tumbled well over his shirt collar. His weapon, a snub-nosed .38 with black electrician's tape wrapped around the grips, was stuck into his waistband at an odd angle.

After he had let me stand there for several uncomfortable minutes, he tossed a set of car keys my way and said, "Go find this in the parking lot, and wait for me." He never looked up from his stack of reports.

"Which car?" I asked.

Now Rinky looked up. "Do I look like your goddamn mother?" he said. "You seem to think you're an investigator. So go fucking investigate and find it."

I found my way out to the parking lot, which was approximately the size of two football fields. There must have been three hundred cars out there—marked, unmarked, covert, what have you. I wandered around clicking the electronic key fob, and eventually a car beeped in response. It was a blue Porsche. I knew at that moment that I was in the perfect place for me.

About a half hour later, Rinky joined me. He slid into the driver's seat, and we were soon in downtown Baltimore. Rinky steered the Porsche down Baltimore Street, otherwise known as "the block." The block consisted of strip clubs, bars, and lots of stumbling drunks. Middle of the morning or middle of the night, the block was not a good place to be. Rinky pulled over. He turned to me, took my gun, my badge, my wallet, and all forms of identification.

Then he handed me forty dollars. "Don't come back until you've bought drugs."

I got out of the Porsche, fighting the urge to run away. I could feel the knots in the pit of my stomach and the tiny hairs on the back of my neck. But this was the job I had hoped for, wasn't it? So I walked the block, looking every inch a fish out of water, and feeling vulnerable without weapon or backup.

Eventually I came to a shabby-looking guy who smelled like the grime covering the tiny alley he occupied. He was an African American of indeterminate age—because of the filth caked on him, he could have been twenty as easily as sixty. But he had what I needed.

I bought some marijuana and a small rock of crack cocaine. When I emerged from the alley between two strip clubs, I spotted the blue Porsche pulled into a spot across the street. I got into the car and handed Rinky the drugs.

"Who'd you buy these from?"

"I don't know," I stammered.

"What did he look like?"

"Uh . . ." I had no idea.

Rinky started laughing. I was so shaken by what I thought was my utter failure that I couldn't tell if he was amused or just being shitty. It didn't really matter—he was laughing at me. I felt like a fool.

When he finally stopped laughing, Rinky said, "Relax, kid. I just wanted to see if you had the guts to buy dope off some fucking scumbag." He then told me that from there on out, if I was going to be any good at this job I would have to pay careful attention to detail. "Detail," he said, "is everything."

We spent the rest of the day at a local watering hole discussing the various aspects of how to be a detective and how to work undercover. Now that I no longer felt so foolish, I realized how much I had loved the adrenaline rush that I had gotten from being on the street armed only with guts, determination, and my own wits. I was eager to absorb everything Rinky could teach me.

Though he was small and extremely laid back, the man was fearless. He was also the most intelligent trooper I ever met. In a heartbeat he could go from blending in with a group of bikers to infiltrating a group of Wall Street stockbrokers, making the transition in the time it took to change his clothes. With a sandwich and a bottle, and after working a sixteen-hour day, Rineker could sit down at midnight in front of his old electric typewriter and write a three-hundred-page wiretap order by the time court opened the next day. You wouldn't find a typo, either. Rineker had the kind of talent that made him a potent adversary to even the best defense attorneys. They couldn't beat his detective work; nor could they manage to get evidence or testimony thrown out at suppression hearings. Rinky's tenacity was what made him exceptional at undercover work. Truly, I learned from the best.

6

I spent the better part of the next fourteen years working narcotics, during which I watched the unit go from "Special Services" to a fully operational Narcotics Division. I began to rise in the ranks, being named 1986 Trooper of the Year. I also married the most amazing woman I had ever met, inheriting her four boys. Soon, our daughter was born.

As sergeant, I supervised several multiagency drug task forces. In that role, I worked with agencies from both city and county, overseeing the deputies and city narcs. I answered to a task force board consisting of chiefs of all these departments. Each of the agencies in the task force had its own policies, and the budgets ranged from adequate to none at all. My job was to blend whatever group of narcs I had into a comprehensive team. Once the cops assigned to me started to refer to themselves as a "task force" instead of referring to themselves as members of their home department, I knew we had built a successful narcotics team.

That was critical. Because of the nature of the work, we had to trust one another—it's that kind of connection that kept us alive. Whenever I was undercover buying drugs, I knew that my teammates were out there with me, conducting surveillance, and that they would dive in without a thought to get me out of any situation that went awry. And they knew I would do the same thing for them if the roles were reversed.

The teams I supervised included the Frederick County narcotics task force and the Metro area task force, which covered Montgomery, Prince George's, and Howard Counties. Our group led the state most years in total number of arrests, as well as drugs and assets seized. The Metro task force was the first in state history to work a case and seize a residence that had been used as a crack house. That day, we served the fourth or fifth search-and-seizure warrant on the house. That being done, we stepped aside, and the United States marshals went in. They cleaned out the house, throwing all the furniture on the curb, boarding the house up, and slapping a sticker on the front door: "Seized by the United States of America, U.S. Marshals Service." The neighbors came out to watch. They clapped and cheered each time another piece of furniture flew out of the house and added to the pile at the curb.

It wasn't long after the task force was up and running that I was appointed a sergeant in the major violators section of the Narcotics Division. Once again I was working and learning directly under the supervision of Detective Sergeant Warren Rineker. Our mission was to identify the sources of the drugs coming into Maryland, collect evidence on them, and make the arrests. These cases were very intense and usually involved a court-ordered wiretap. We would work the case forward and backward, looking for clues and evidence to cement the prosecution's case. Some of these cases would take twelve to eighteen months to complete. Despite the complexities, we never lost a wiretap investigation in court. Under Rinky's guidance, we did things in a big way. Instead of seizing thousands of dollars and ounces of cocaine, we seized hundreds of thousands of dollars and multiple kilos of cocaine and heroin.

So it was a shock when, after nearly a decade and a half in narcotics, I was informed that my tenure in the division had run its course. New command staff coming in had concluded that there were several of us who had been in the division too long. We were reassigned. Soon I found myself back in uniform working as a sergeant at the Waterloo Barrack, located west of Baltimore in Howard County. My first day back I was to report to Waterloo at 7 a.m. I had spent several hours the night before making sure that my uniform was squared away, meaning that all collar ornaments, name tag, badge, and ribbons for my awards were properly placed. Of course the uniform was newly pressed, with military creases down the sleeves. Once again, I was determined to look like I had stepped out of a recruiting poster. This attitude was a source of pride for state police forces, but I have to admit that I wasn't really feeling it that day.

And then my knack for falling into cases practically greeted me at the door.

I had stopped by the barrack the day before to pick up the marked cruiser that had been assigned to me. Now, as I was leaving Frederick County about 5:30 a.m. in car A-24, headed for my first day of work at Waterloo Barrack, I was wondering how I was going to do as a shift supervisor, primarily confined to the barrack as the duty officer. I was used to the front lines, and I wasn't looking forward to being stuck in the barrack behind a desk.

As I steered my cruiser onto I-70 going east that morning, I came up behind a small car. The car stood out—it was being driven in the fast lane, traveling about thirty-five miles per hour in the posted fifty-five- miles-per-hour zone. As I came up behind it, I noticed the driver was alone. Also, it was clear that, even at that slow speed, he was having a difficult time keeping the car on the road. Great. I hadn't made a DUI traffic stop and arrest in more than fourteen years. "Just like riding a bike," I muttered.

I called the traffic stop in over the radio, which was silent. There was nothing happening in Howard County on a Wednesday morning as far as the state police were concerned. The night shift crew was likely at the barrack finishing their paperwork from the night and week before, getting ready for their long weekend. I looked at my watch—it was still too early for the day shift to be on the road.

I activated the emergency equipment on A-24 and gave the guy a short little blast of the siren. The driver slowly steered left off the paved portion of the interstate and stopped at a sort of a cocked angle in the grassy center median.

It's funny how at that moment all those lessons Corporal Cameron had taught me years before immediately came back to me. I parked A-24 at an offset angle, then got out of the cruiser and cautiously walked up to the stopped vehicle. I spoke to the driver, who was either drunk, high, or both. The guy was well past fifty years old and was barely able to keep his eyes open.

I glanced in beside him at a small gym bag sitting on the empty passenger seat. My senses were on alert—what was in that bag? It could have been anything from gym clothes to a semiautomatic weapon. I asked for his driver's license and registration card. While he looked for it, I talked to him, trying to get him to engage in conversation. Partly I wanted to hear the proof of his intoxicated state. But I also wanted him focused on something besides trying to hurt me.

When he couldn't produce a license, I got him out of the vehicle and went through the standard sobriety test. He failed miserably, so I placed him under arrest. When I searched him, I found a small baggie in one of his pockets—a small rock of crack cocaine. I asked him if he had any more drugs or anything that would hurt me. He stared at me, glassy eyed. Slurring his words, he said, "It's only for my own personal use, but there is a little more crack in the gym bag, plus a gun, and some cash that I won at the casino."

A little more crack—I removed almost a quarter pound of cocaine, a handgun with the serial numbers filed off, and more than $10,000 in cash from the gym bag. Here was my first uniformed felony arrest in more than fourteen years. I had seized a large amount of money and a car and a gun, and I hadn't yet made it to the barrack for my first shift.

7

All my years of experience, including investigating homicides, was about to be sorely tested by this apparent sniper case. For one thing, it's a rule of thumb in homicides that the most critical time to obtain evidence is the first twenty-four hours after a murder is discovered. Yet the sniper shootings were occurring so rapidly that the well-established rules of thumb had to be thrown out the window. Investigators had to make plans on the fly.

But no matter how well a police department trains and plans in advance, initial confusion at the crime scene is part of the job, and that confusion has to be managed. The best way to manage it is for every one of us to stay in our own lane, so to speak, to concentrate on doing our job regardless of what's happening around us. We have to have faith that the uniformed police who are usually the first responders have been trained to secure the crime scene. They will quickly assess the situation and determine the total scene scope. Then, if possible, they will double or triple the size of the scene and secure it with crime scene tape, or whatever means are available. Access to the scene must be strictly limited so that it's not contaminated by citizens, or even other police officers, who just want a look for themselves. The first responding units will start a crime scene log to indicate who entered the scene, the date and time in and out, and the role or reason for everyone entering. The log should also include any other appropriate factors, such as weather conditions, and must be maintained by the first responding officer until he or she is relieved by proper authority.

There are numerous factors that can complicate a crime scene, such as where it's located. Is it in a public area? Is it outside or inside? If it's outside, the weather can have an enormous influence on the crime scene investigation and what evidence is collected and how quickly.

From the moment the murder is discovered and reported, the initial lead investigator and the investigative team must come up to speed as quickly as possible. Potential witnesses need to be quickly identified and kept separated until they are interviewed. Investigators also need to quickly debrief the uniformed officers and the medical first responders to get a handle on who they are, what they saw when they arrived, what witnesses or victims may have told them, as well as any other critical information, including facts that no one may recognize as important until later. Formal statements must be taken to confirm what the witnesses saw, heard, or claimed they saw. It's important to get these statements as quickly and as accurately as possible, while the events are fresh in the witnesses' minds.

Moreover, different witnesses may require a different investigative skill set during the interview, based on how traumatized they may be and any language barrier that might exist. Investigators must quickly determine who the victim is, what he or she was doing in the location where the crime occurred, how the victim was killed, and if there are any obvious reasons, such as a robbery that may have gone bad, that could point to a motive. All these steps must be taken before the real in-depth investigation can start.

This requires a dedicated team all working together—from the uniformed patrol officer who caught the initial call, to the crime scene or lab people who collect the evidence, to the investigators charged with investigating the crime and tracking down the killer. As the complexity of the case increases, so does the number of investigators and other stakeholders who become involved. This takes time, coordination, and resources.

So when the rapid succession of shootings and killings began in October 2002, the Montgomery County police quickly became overwhelmed. They simply didn't have enough resources to cover all the crime scenes, let alone to overcome the initial confusion or to make sense out of what was happening to their community. The Montgomery County Police Department is a very experienced, very professional, and highly motivated department, but no one agency alone could have gotten on top of so many shootings occurring so quickly. Other police departments around the country may have claimed *they* could have handled it, but having lived and seen firsthand how complex this case was, I know better.

The October 2 shooting murder of James Martin in the parking lot of a Shoppers Food Warehouse in Wheaton was still in its initial phase of investigation when the murders and chaos of October 3 began. At 7:41 a.m. James Buchanan was cutting grass along the street around a large car dealership in Rockville. When the parking lot attendant found him, he was lying on the car lot with the mower tilted over a few feet away. He had died for no apparent reason. As police and emergency medical responders arrived and transported Buchanan to the hospital, passersby debated whether he had slipped and fallen under the running mower, or whether the motor had exploded. The confusion continued as medical personnel at Suburban Hospital initially diagnosed his death as an industrial accident.

Then, at 8:12 a.m., at a Mobil Gas Station in Aspen Hill, Montgomery County, a few minutes from where Buchanan had fallen, Premkumar Walekar was pumping gas into his taxi cab when he was shot. Once again, the death had no apparent motive. There was no robbery or attempted robbery, no reasonable explanation as to why he was shot. He just seemed to be in the wrong place at the wrong time.

A bystander flagged down a Montgomery County patrol officer, so police responded to Walekar's homicide first, having not yet been dispatched to the auto dealership where Buchanan was killed. Three murders had been committed in Montgomery County in a little more than a seventeen-hour time frame. But nothing connected any of these instances. Not yet. And there was about to be a fourth.

At 8:37 a.m. Sarah Ramos was sitting on a park bench in front of a Crisp and Juicy Chicken restaurant in Silver Spring, waiting for a bus, when she was struck in the head by a bullet. This was in a busy strip mall in a densely populated area during the busiest time of day.

It was just a few blocks from where Walekar had been killed just twenty-five minutes earlier.

A passing motorist called the Montgomery County Police Department to report a suicide. Once uniformed officers arrived on the scene, however, suicide was quickly ruled out. At that moment the officers realized that their county was under attack, yet they had no idea who was causing the carnage or how to stop it. The quick determination of facts showed no connection among any of the victims. This left the possibility of some sort of gang-related motivation, since there were several violent gangs known to be operating in and around Montgomery County.

However, since these shootings were just a year after September 11, and some six months after the anthrax case, terrorism immediately went to the top of the list. This is when the Montgomery County Police Department began reaching out to allied agencies, including the Maryland State Police.

8

When Sarah Ramos was killed, I was sitting in my office in Columbia, Maryland, oblivious of the events unfolding in Montgomery County. The first hint came when Montgomery County police put out a lookout for a white van occupied by two men. As I would later learn, a landscaper working close to where Ramos was murdered said he had seen a white van with two men in it leaving the parking lot immediately after the shooting, heading north. Two men. It was the first time anyone had had any hint that this wasn't a lone gunman. The BOLO (be on the lookout) went out to all surrounding counties and smaller police departments, as well as to the D.C. Metropolitan Police Department and the troopers assigned to the Rockville Barrack.

Though forensic analysis was not yet available, it was obvious to any trained investigator that the high-speed bullets fired were from a rifle. That meant one thing—a sniper. But it was only speculation as to why it was occurring. Speculation was something there wasn't any time for—the immediate problem was trying to stop the killing. The only way police could think to do that was to flood the area with as many police officers as possible. The hope was that officers would get lucky and catch the shooters, or at least make it difficult for them to continue their killing spree. Nothing was concrete, though. Police were still trying to figure out connections among the victims, and trying to locate a motive. Plus, they were being cautious; there was no indication this van had any connection to the shootings. It could still be just one shooter.

At 9:58 a.m. Lori Ann Lewis-Rivera was vacuuming the inside of her minivan at a Shell gas station several miles from the Crisp and Juicy. At that same moment I was in the midst of being briefed about the shootings by Major Jimmy Ballard. As I listened, I was trying to wrap my head around the events. My mind was racing—I had to form a plan, issue orders, and get the troops and the agency mobilized and moving.

Because things were happening faster than the police could keep up with them, news about the killings had not been made public. We didn't want to inform the public until we had enough information and a clearer picture of what was going on. So, as Lewis-Rivera went about her task unaware of what was going on in the area, she was murdered. As with the other killings, she appeared to be in the wrong place at the wrong time.

There were no witnesses. Security footage recovered from the gas station and surrounding businesses captured the moment when she was struck by the bullet, but there was nothing on the video that was of any evidentiary value, nothing to help identify any suspects or suspect vehicles. We decided to set up the state police temporary command post at the Rockville Barrack in an effort to coordinate all the active homicide investigations and activity associated around the multiple crime scenes. The Montgomery County Police Department was now scrambling for clues to who was doing the shooting and why. Until they understood motive or had more evidence, they were powerless to stop it. All they could do was respond to the violence as it unfolded around them.

As a precaution, and because of what had occurred at Columbine High School in Colorado, all the schools in Montgomery County were placed on Code Blue alert and locked down. Outdoor activities associated with the schools were canceled. Through dribs and drabs, the public was beginning to learn that something serious and violent was happening in their normally quiet community.

I was on the road between my office and the Rockville Barrack when I got a call on my cell phone about Lori Ann Lewis-Rivera's murder. Meanwhile, everyone—including, now, me—was on the lookout for a white box truck or a white van. I knew the state police wouldn't be involved with the investigation beyond providing manpower and support, but still, the investigator in me began processing what limited information I had in an effort to understand what was happening and why. Was this really a lone gunman? Or was this some sort of terrorist cell or cells carrying out a sophisticated mission? Was this the other shoe that we had all expected to drop after 9/11? It sure felt like it. A sniper out there killing random people was a nightmare scenario for cops, especially in light of 9/11. Were there other groups, in other cities, carrying out the same type of mission? Was there a connection between the victims that would make some sort of twisted sense once we knew it? If so, who was going to be next?

I was trying to put myself in the mind-set of the bad guys, which is what I had been trained to do. If indeed this were the work of a terrorist cell, the next logical step would be to take out a law enforcement officer or two. The seeds of panic would have already been planted in the general public, so now it would make sense to target cops. That would show that the police department and the government weren't able to protect the public. Was this another act of war perpetrated on our country? Was the new front line Montgomery County?

It all made terrible sense to me as I sped toward Rockville Barrack. I thought about the dozens of troopers around the region and the state who would have their duties and barrack assignments shifted to Montgomery County to assist in this investigation. I thought about the fact that all the victims were shot with a high-speed bullet, which meant a high-powered rifle, which meant that the ballistic bullet-proof vests the troopers wore weren't going to stop that type of bullet. Those vests would be just another piece of clothing that would have to be removed at the hospital, or, worse, the morgue.

I knew that one of the easiest and first mistakes you could make in any homicide investigation was to get tunnel vision—to decide in your own mind why the crime has been committed and who the most likely suspect might be, then to fashion the evidence to fit the scenario in your head. Was this what I was starting to do? There had to be some rational, albeit twisted reason why this was happening and why these particular people had been chosen. Was this a street gang hit or a major drug-trafficking operation that had somehow gone bad, and all our victims were somehow intertwined in it? Were they collateral damage, getting in the way of a bullet intended for somebody else? Or was this the worst kind of case—a sniper running loose killing people at random simply because he could? Whatever it was, this was a real who-the-hell-done-it case, one that was going to be extremely difficult to solve unless the perpetrator or perpetrators made a mistake. Or, through his or their own arrogance, pointed us in the right direction.

From I-95 South I caught the Washington Beltway and headed west to I-270, which led north to the Rockville Barrack. The BOLO for the white van or box truck was being rebroadcast about every fifteen minutes. The Maryland State Police operates communications among all of its cars using multiple radio frequencies. Because of my position, I was lucky enough to have a newer radio that could broadcast on the channel or barrack area I was traveling in, but could scan the other channels as well. The primary channel overrode the scanning function—any radio traffic coming from the barrack that the radio was switched to would be heard loud and clear. To the untrained ear, it would be like listening to an AM radio station near dark; you pick up multiple stations on one setting. It can sound confusing and impossible to understand at times. Most state troopers take cars home and can use them for their personal and family use, within reason. My wife hated that radio because it was always squawking and was turned up loud. To her, it was an annoying amount of meaningless noise. To me, it was perfectly clear what was being broadcast.

I switched over from the Waterloo channel onto the Forestville channel (Prince George's County), then onto the Rockville channel. The airwaves were full of news of troopers stopping every white van and box-style truck on the highway. Troopers ride alone. Since there's only one trooper needed for one riot, as our motto had it, why should we change? There were many old salts who still thought this way. But I always lent a hand whenever I could. If I saw a trooper on the side of the road on a traffic stop, I always pulled in behind him or stopped across the road if we were going in opposite directions. This was to make sure the trooper was okay, and also to send a signal to the driver who had been stopped that the trooper had backup. On my way to Rockville that day I pulled up behind several troopers. Now, more than ever, troopers needed someone watching their backs.

9

By the time I got to Rockville Barrack, I had worked up a head of steam. I was angry that somebody was out there bushwhacking citizens with no obvious reason or motive. But that anger had to wait. There were troopers heading here from all over the state, and they needed to be brought up to speed. As they arrived, I briefed them with what little information we had. The case was still very much in the initial phase, and the Maryland State Police had yet to be given any specific assignments.

Captain McAndrew and senior leadership were tasked with the responsibility of contacting the Montgomery County police chief, Charles Moose, and his investigative team to determine what, specifically, the state police were being requested to do. One thing I knew for sure: the killers weren't going to show up at the Rockville Barrack to turn themselves in. So it did absolutely no good to have thirty or forty extra troopers and their rollers sitting in the barrack parking lot.

As the troopers trickled into the barrack, I briefed them in small groups before sending them back out on the road. "Here's what we know," I told them. "The shooters are using some type of high-speed bullet, most likely from a long gun or an assault-type weapon. Your vests likely won't stop this bullet."

A few troopers exchanged glances, but they all stood fast.

"If this is a terrorist attack, law enforcement are likely targets. It would be a way for them to further drive panic in the community and among our ranks."

The room was silent, but the troopers were resolute. They knew the risks and understood what they were being asked to do. They understood that they were outgunned and had to play by rules, while the shooter could kill at will. But no one expressed any reservations. Every one of them willingly headed out.

I instructed them to concentrate mainly on the interstate highways: I-270 and the Beltway, as well as State Route 355. All the murders had taken place along the 355 corridor. I wanted our troopers to be everywhere, visible, and making their presence known by stopping every white van, white box truck, or any other vehicle they deemed suspicious or out of place. My hope was that the heavy police patrol would get these killers to lie low for a while, giving us time to sort things out and come up with a plan.

I told the troopers to call out every traffic stop to the barrack communications officer. "Make sure you know exactly where you are," I said, "and for god's sake, back each other up out there."

As the deadly morning of October 3 turned to afternoon, the shootings ceased. Maybe our strategy was working. Using this gift of time, we contacted the FBI and the ATF—the federal Bureau of Alcohol, Tobacco, Firearms and Explosives—to get them involved. Since the ATF had a lab in the area, they agreed to make their ballistic experts available, and the sniper case was made a lab priority. It was during that unexpectedly quiet afternoon that one of the bullets recovered from the numerous crime scenes was identified. It was a high-velocity .223-caliber round. A ballistics match was going to take a little time, but it wasn't going to be a stretch to assume that all the bullets recovered to this point in the investigation likely came from the same rifle.

Once all the troopers had been briefed, I was sent over to Montgomery County police headquarters to assist in answering telephone calls and working tips that had already started to flood the police station. As I pulled up to Montgomery County HQ, I saw several news trucks parked outside. Obviously the case was no longer a secret. But the news crews could help spread the word. The public needed to know that we were actively stopping every white van and truck on the road.

I was escorted into the building and directed upstairs to a smallish second-floor room, a combination conference room and bullpen area for the county's Criminal Investigation Unit. At least twenty cops were crammed into this space that had been designed for six or seven investigators. Phones were ringing, police radios were on high volume, everyone was talking at once. Cops on phones took notes, answered questions, processed information from cops in the field, and fielded inquiries from other police agencies in the tristate area.

I pulled up a folding chair and started answering calls. I had no clue what questions I needed to ask. None of us did. All we knew was what we had heard on the police radio and in news reports on commercial radio and TV. I was working at a folding table—the kind you would see in a church community room—along with five or six other cops. Several telephones had been pulled from somewhere and plugged into a multiple phone jack. The cord stretched over the table, under a desk, and across the floor. A fistful of tip sheets had been shoved in front of me, and I got to work.

My first call was from a woman in North Carolina who was convinced that her ex-husband was the shooter. She said her ex was a violent man with a long, violent criminal record. He was a white supremacist and owned multiple high-powered rifles and firearms, even though it was a federal offense for a convicted felon to be in possession of any guns. She was sure it was her ex because she hadn't seen him for several days. As she put it, he had always wanted to go to Washington and kill all the "niggers that had led the country down the toilet." He owned a white van, she said. I took down all the investigative information, including his date of birth, address, and physical description.

After I hung up, I ran a quick check on the guy in the numerous state and national databases. Just as the caller had said, her ex had a long, violent criminal history. He also owned a white van and was a known member of a white supremacist group. "This asshole," I said to nobody in particular, "is a real shithead and needs to be at the top of the list for no other reason than who he is." I looked around to find someone to give the information to, but every cop in the room was taking calls and getting info very much like what I had just gotten. Reluctantly, I placed my notes in a box and moved on to the next call.

Several hours later, I had to take a break. As I walked down the hall looking for a restroom and a soda machine, a man approached me. "Chief Moose," he said. We shook hands, and he thanked me for helping and said he wanted to make sure I had taken the time to eat. Chief Moose looked like a man who was used to an orderly world. Now that it was turned upside down, I suspect he was trying to process what had happened and what needed to be done. As I shook his hand, it was as though I could hear what he was thinking—maybe because we were all thinking it.

Things were out of control, and everybody was looking to him to provide leadership and come up with a plan. The burden of command can be extremely heavy, and there was no training in the world that he—or any of us, for that matter—could have obtained during a career that would have prepared him for a situation like this. I immediately liked him. If he took the time to make sure a borrowed trooper had eaten, he cared about his cops.

As the afternoon shadows grew long, we were beginning to

realize that this investigation wasn't going to end quickly. In one day, we had saturated the area with law enforcement, but now we had to be prepared to keep that up. Maryland State Police first sergeants around the state were ordered to look at their staffing, cut their commands down to bare minimums, and send troopers to Montgomery County to work round the clock. Leave and vacations were canceled. Troopers were placed on twelve-hour shifts in an effort to keep as many on the road as possible. Because of the multiple killings, troopers were on edge and being very deliberate during their traffic stops. Some motorists had been stopped several times—in the morning as they traveled to work and then again in late afternoon or early evening on their way home from work. For the most part, the general public was very cooperative. Everyone understood that the police were looking for heavily armed killers. As a result, the public seemed to accept the curt, direct orders they were given by the officers and troopers who had stopped them.

By the end of that day, the ATF identified the bullets as likely coming from the same rifle, suspected to be a Bushmaster .223-caliber assault weapon. It was known to be very accurate and, in the hands of a skilled shooter, extremely deadly. That gave us another clue: the shooter did possess a skill set. It's easy to take a rifle like that to a range and hit a nonmoving paper target from a great distance. But it's much harder to look down the barrel of the rifle and get a person in your sights, and then be steady enough to squeeze the trigger.

But that's all we knew. We still didn't know if we were dealing with a local psychopath on a onetime rampage or an organized terrorist cell that was bent on terrorizing the area. Considering what had happened over the past year, we were thinking it was the latter.

It wasn't until later that night that I heard what the public was hearing. Around 7 p.m., I checked in with my wife. It was all over the news, she said. News channels were breaking into regular programming about every fifteen minutes with some piece of information. I told her what I knew and what I had been doing. "They may send us home around eight to get some rest," I said. "But I'll have to be back at it early tomorrow."

When 8 p.m. came, I headed north on I-270 into Frederick County and home. Despite being exhausted, I couldn't stop going over things. Even though I wasn't yet deeply involved in the investigation, and the state police's role thus far was nothing more than to flood the area with law enforcement, my mind was turning over each scenario, looking for connections, for some way to make sense out of all this. Was this going to continue? Were there going to be more killings? Was there some sort of rational explanation for these irrational acts? As I pulled into my driveway, I hadn't come up with a thing.

I was tired. It has always been difficult for me to turn it off when I got home. Still, I did my best not to bring the job home. Jean gets that, doesn't bring up the job unless I opened up to her first. That night, things happened in blurry snippets. My daughter was telling me about what had happened at cheerleading practice, and I tried to concentrate, to hear what she was telling me. Then Jean told me about her day, her voice light and soothing. It was her way of bringing me home mentally. The TV was on and we were all half watching whatever show was on.

Then suddenly the show was interrupted by breaking news from Washington, D.C. There had been another murder. Pascal Charlot was walking down the street on Georgia Avenue near Kalmia Road about 9:30 p.m., just beyond the Maryland state line in D.C., when he was struck by a high-speed bullet. Charlot was killed instantly. He had no connection to any of the other victims.

According to the news report, Metropolitan Police responded to the scene, arriving within minutes. Witnesses claimed the shot came from across the street, where there was a chest-high cinder-block wall hidden by pine trees and bushes. Another witness reported seeing a blue four-door Chevy Caprice driving casually away from the scene with its lights off.

10

Friday, October 4, 2002. Before leaving for home the night before, I had been assigned to report to a local National Guard armory at 5 a.m. The armory is several miles from Montgomery County Police headquarters and fairly centrally located to all the shooting locations. Troopers, including criminal investigators, narcs, and my own Intelligence Division troopers were being reassigned from headquarters to the armory. They were to report by 5:30 a.m. I was to brief them and hand out assignments.

I had not gotten much rest in the few hours I'd had. The events of the day before had kept invading my sleep. I've always worn my emotions on my sleeve. Even though we were taught in the academy not to take our jobs personally, I can't operate that way. Every crime I have ever investigated is personal. It has always felt good to slap the cuffs on the bad guys, if for no other reason than to make sure they understand that they didn't get away with it. To me, it is my personal responsibility to look under the bed and kick that monster hiding there right in the teeth. Whoever it was that was killing citizens at random, *that* was now the monster under the bed. I wanted to do everything in my ability to drag that monster out. Lying in bed pretending to sleep wasn't accomplishing that. I was angry, as was every cop in Maryland and D.C. that night.

The killing of Pascal Charlot opened another can of worms as far as the investigation was concerned. In addition to bringing in the D.C. Metropolitan Police by extending the shootings across the state line, it also officially brought the resources of the federal government and federal law enforcement agencies into the investigation. As I had sat watching the late news in total disbelief, once again the thought of some organized terrorist cell preyed on my mind. This was the only rational explanation I could come up with. Were there multiple sniper teams operating in the area? What were we up against? I believed that these were well-trained and organized killers hiding in plain sight. One thing was sure. This was not going to stop until we stopped them, and there were likely going to be more people dying at their hand. So far, all law enforcement had been able to do was show up at each scene with another body bag.

Before I had turned off the TV, Captain McAndrew had called to make sure I was aware of what had happened and to inform me that the D.C. Metropolitan Police were working the case and Montgomery County detectives were on their way to the District to compare notes and join the investigations. Our plan hashed out for the next day hadn't changed. Since I was not a primary investigator, I wasn't privy to all the investigative details. That was frustrating. But my mission was to provide support at this point, and to have our troopers working as a team to do our best to suppress the killings.

I was awake and dressed by 3:30 a.m. As I did every day, I checked my weapon before heading to work, only this day I double- and triple-checked it. A trooper never knows when his sidearm slides into the holster if it will be for the last time. It's part of the job, and that day I couldn't help but wonder. I wasn't afraid, but we were up against an enemy that had proven their ability to kill from long distance without hesitation. This wasn't like any other foe I had ever encountered.

I made a point to kiss my wife goodbye. She was awake, and stirred as I kissed her. We embraced, and it seemed like she held on a little longer than usual. I don't know for sure what she was thinking, but she understands what we in law enforcement face. She understands how her trooper thinks, and knows his dedication and tenacity. I also looked in on my daughter. As I watched her sleep, it reaffirmed my reasons for being in law enforcement. I wondered what kind of world she would be growing up in: a safe and carefree one, or one in which terrorism had changed the fiber of the culture?

Even though my shift started at 5 a.m., I arrived at my assigned location by 4:15. Those troopers not in uniform had been instructed to go to the National Guard armory in Rockville to get their assignments; uniformed troopers had been directed to the Rockville Barrack to receive theirs. The uniforms were going to be doing pretty much the same thing they had done the day before, except there were now close to one hundred troopers working the area. At least one trooper had been assigned to each school in the county, to patrol the area. The other troopers were to continue aggressive patrol on the interstate and Route 355, which all evidence suggested might be the primary killing zone for the sniper.

Captain McAndrew was already at the armory when I arrived. He was going over the list of nonuniform troopers we had to work with. He looked like he'd had about as much sleep as I had. Over the next hour, criminal investigators, narcs, and other nonuniformed personnel arrived from all over the state. Some of them had driven more than three hours to get to the briefing.

The tension in the big classroom was now thick, and the troopers wore it like skin. There was some apprehension about the fact that a lot of these troopers had never worked in Montgomery County before and weren't familiar with the area. Still, they were troopers, and troopers follow orders. So they were all there ready to take on whatever assignment came their way.

McAndrew briefed us all on what had occurred the day and the evening before. We were told that there was nothing new to report as far as what or who we were looking for. The odd thing about that was that a BOLO for a blue Caprice had been broadcast over the Metropolitan Police radio the night before, yet law enforcement in Maryland never received that message. In Maryland, we were still focusing on a white box truck or van.

The best information we had was that our suspects were possibly two guys in a white box truck or van, and that they were armed with at least one rifle and had demonstrated a kill-at-will pattern. Our assignments for the day: move around the Route 355 corridor and conduct surveillance in and around shopping centers, parking lots, and gas stations. Those of us who drove unmarked rollers (easily identified as police cars being driven by police officers) were told to be visible at all times in order to help ease the growing public apprehension. The undercover guys in covert vehicles were to concentrate on trying to spot anybody suspicious, out of place, or who appeared to be casing a location.

That was the plan. It was just a stopgap measure, intended to get as many cops on the street as possible. As for the investigative plan, it was still being formed. The feds were coming into the investigation, and the entire operation was in need of serious organization. Meanwhile, the rest of us needed strong communication, and that was still a problem. The Montgomery County police had assigned the state police as many handheld radios as they could spare, but there still weren't enough to go around. We divided the radios among us so that anything new being broadcast over the Montgomery County police radio could be relayed to us.

After being briefed and assigned areas, the troopers hit the road. I didn't have any specific assignment. My job was to make sure I could respond to the barrack or Montgomery County Police Department headquarters if needed. I was on the road by 5:30. I stayed in the Rockville area, driving slowly and observing everything. I tried to get into the heads of the shitheads; I drove to all the locations of the killings, with the exception of the one in the District. I wanted to get a feel for the crime scenes and, more important, a feel for the surroundings. If the targets were not specific based on who they were or the color of their skin, and they had no connection to one another, then the killer or killers were looking for environments that were easy to stalk, and where a target would be vulnerable.

At each location, I was struck by the number of people out and about. From that, it would be easy to think that the killings hadn't deterred people from their everyday habits; but I saw different. From my vantage point, I noticed that as people parked and exited their cars, they looked around much more than usual. They weren't lingering in the parking lot or strolling along casually. People walked with purpose; they took no time to stand in a parking lot for idle chat. They went directly to the building where they were going or went directly to their cars and got in as soon as they could get the doors open. The killers were already inside their heads.

About the locations themselves, I noticed that in each case there was a parking lot either at the scene, beside it, or across the street. All the shootings were close to the street, so that the killers could make their shot quickly and get out of the area easily—well before the police would have a chance to respond. Judging by the places they chose, the killers weren't looking to take on the police right now. Still, I was confident that a trooper or police officer who appeared on the scene would be in grave danger: if the circumstances were right, the killers would take the shot.

Each shopping center, parking lot, or convenience store I came to, I entered slowly, trying to spot areas where I would go if I were the stalker. I studied sight lines, angles, and visibility. Then I watched. How could a killer blend in? Where could he hide? How would he leave the area quickly and quietly after taking the shot? When I decided what I would do and where I would go if I lived in their sick little world, then those were the areas of parking lots that I concentrated on, looking for anything, or anyone carrying something that would have been about the right length as a rifle. Every white van or box truck that came into view I watched intently. It's amazing how many were on the road. With each stop I made and each area I surveilled, I was hopeful—maybe I would get lucky. But I was also realistic enough to know it was a very slim chance.

By early afternoon, the ATF had bullets and fragments in four of the seven shootings. The ATF confirmed that they had come from the same .223-caliber assault rifle, likely a Bushmaster.

Then, at 2:30 that afternoon, Caroline Seawell came out of a Michaels craft store in the Spotsylvania Mall in Fredericksburg, Virginia, thirty-five miles south of Washington. As she loaded her bags into the back of her minivan, a high-speed bullet struck her in the back. She was badly wounded. A witness told police that he saw a white van fleeing the scene. Another witness reported seeing a dark, older-model Chevrolet slowly exiting the mall moments after the shooting.

Thanks to this new shooting, the case had now expanded to two states and the D.C. area. Virginia authorities and the Virginia State Police were now involved in the case. The search area had just grown exponentially. The snipers appeared to be heading south. Also, this was the second shooting incident at a Michaels craft store—the first one was the shot fired through the window of a Michaels store two nights before. Another commonality: two of the victims had been driving minivans. Was this some sick attack on the stereotypical soccer mom?

11

Prior to the Virginia shooting, I had been reassigned to the Montgomery County police headquarters. The infrastructure of the investigation was beginning to take shape. Tip calls were coming in by the hundreds and were already to the point of being unmanageable. I was put in charge of a team of troopers, along with state police civilian analysts and crime analysts from Montgomery County, to try to get a handle on the number of tips and leads that were coming in.

After the April 1995 Oklahoma City bombing killed 168 people and injured 650 more, the FBI developed a tip-tracking program called Rapid Start. It was designed to manage all the calls offering leads. Like this sniper case, the Oklahoma City bombing triggered thousands of calls and tips, flooding local and federal crime solvers and tip lines.

Tips come in from all sorts of people with all types of motives for making those calls. Some people may have seen something they thought was suspicious, or they may know somebody who could be responsible. We get calls from people who say that God has spoken to them, and, depending on how much media attention a case has drawn, we also hear from people who believe they have psychic skills and want to help us solve the case. Tip calls often come in from people who have a score to settle with a neighbor, an ex-spouse, a former employer. And then there are the calls from the people I call the "confessors." As the sniper case grew ever bigger as a media story, we got more and more people calling to confess to all the shootings.

Whatever the motivation, police encourage these calls. Information about a crime is often difficult to find. Investigators never know which small piece of information, that by itself may appear unimportant, could turn a case around. Most homicides, robberies, and burglaries affect a small sphere of people, so because there are fewer calls, the tips received are easily managed. But when a big case comes along, complete with heavy press coverage, tips pour in by the thousands. In such a case, viable information can easily be lost or overlooked. To prevent that, every single tip must be recorded and evaluated to determine if it is (a) useful and (b) actionable. No tip is discarded; future evidence could benefit from something that seems unrelated today.

All of this takes people and time. All too often, however, law enforcement doesn't have enough people to handle the volume of calls. In the sniper case, we had zero time. The snipers were still out there, still killing. And now the terror had expanded throughout the entire mid-Atlantic region.

Prior to Oklahoma City, the system for vetting information was nothing more than paper and pen and piles of tip sheets. Rapid Start was a major improvement for large-case management. Operators answering tip lines could enter the information directly into the program as the tips were received. The tips could then be numbered, tracked, and managed, with a clear log of what, if any, action was taken or required for each tip. Rapid Start also helped to ensure that nothing was lost. Even so, Rapid Start had its short-comings. It was able to organize and store the information, but it didn't have the ability to conduct link analysis. An investigator still had to manually go through the information received to determine if it had any relevance to the investigation.

Link analysis is simply what its name implies: linking bits of information, such as names, evidence, times, places, who was seen where and when, in relation to events that occurred around the time and place of each of the homicides and shootings. Were there common threads among all these events? Link analysis can be accomplished by a trained investigator or analyst, but it is impossible for one person to have access to thousands of pieces of information coming in twenty-four hours a day. Therefore, multiple analysts are required. Often, they are working independently from one another. More than one set of eyes and ears involved in the process lends itself to yet another problem.

Multiple analysts working a case often don't know what information another analyst working the same case has. This lack of cohesion spreads as more tips come in and more analysts become involved. To avoid or prevent this, an investigative team or intelligence unit is brought in to coordinate information through a chain-of-command structure. Information and intelligence are vetted and assigned relevancy. One person or one small group will have knowledge of the case and will be in constant contact with the lead investigative team. That was my job, working along with Captain McAndrew.

Once Rapid Start was deployed in this case, all backlogged tips that had come in over the past thirty-plus hours were entered into the system, and all tip line and call center locations downloaded the Rapid Start program. But in time we started referring to it as Rapid Stop. Now, instead of our going out and looking for the proverbial needle in a haystack in multiple fields *full* of haystacks, those haystacks were being brought to us and dumped in our laps. But we still didn't know if we had the right haystacks, or even the right field.

By late afternoon that October 4, the Montgomery County police headquarters was a mass of both cops and confusion. The headquarters simply wasn't designed to house the two hundred to three hundred police officers and federal agents now packed into the offices and corridors. Any outsider looking in would have thought there was no order at all, nobody in charge, and that the police didn't know what they were doing. But this investigation was roughly thirty-six hours old. Police operations in Montgomery County had gone from a relative normal operation to a command center with hundreds of agents from the FBI, the ATF, the U.S. Marshals Service, the Maryland State Police, and now the Virginia State Police. We had been thrown together to form what would become one of the most effective joint criminal investigative teams in U.S. history.

Although there had been casual relationships between law enforcement officers from the various agencies and departments, none of us had ever experienced this type of close working relationship. It crossed agency lines, which required that we trust one another. Were we ready for that?

———

The man in charge of making that happen was Captain Bernie Forsyth, the lead investigator. Forsyth, a senior veteran of the Montgomery County Police Department, was a longtime criminal investigator, and his reputation was outstanding. Patient yet determined, Forsyth was a perfect choice to lead the investigation. I had known him from my days working narcotics. Because narcotics, theft, and burglary cases frequently involve the same suspects committing crimes to fund their habits, Captain Forsyth and I had crossed paths several times over the years. He was a no-bullshit guy who cared about solving cases and getting bad guys off the street. I liked the guy—I was wired the same way.

But seeing him at headquarters that afternoon, I felt sorry for him. He looked shell-shocked, but determined. Cops like Bernie Forsyth are driven; they do this job so the shitheads and scumbags don't win. When we win, we believe there is nothing our agency can't handle. This case was different, though. This was uncharted territory. We felt blindfolded. It even felt different in the command center. Unlike many cases, when agencies tussle over who is in charge, none of us cared. We knew this was going to have to be a team effort.

By 6 p.m., there was no more news to report. Investigators from the Virginia State Police and the local sheriff's department were still working the Seawell crime scene, but we were no closer to knowing who was responsible than we had been when this all had started. Because the case had jumped state lines, the media attention had mushroomed. TV trucks and news crews surrounded Montgomery police headquarters, and the case was now a constant topic of discussion on Fox and CNN. Plus, there was a growing concern that the media area surrounding police headquarters would be an excellent, easy target. We still didn't know the snipers' motivation. If the purpose was to cause panic, taking out a TV news personality would have served that purpose. Streets surrounding the headquarters were sealed off, and counter-sniper teams were deployed. Because local and state police forces were maxed out, this job fell on the U.S. Marshals Service.

That evening, Montgomery County police headquarters was a madhouse of cops in motion. Uniform officers were coming and going, and the growing investigative teams were elbow to elbow. Phones were ringing, and it was becoming more and more difficult to hear the voice on the other end of the line when you did answer the telephone. We needed more room and a quiet place where the intelligence team could work.

The federal agencies were already on it, trying to locate a space to rent. It had to accommodate one thousand officers and have conference rooms, space for working groups, and room for uniformed officers to be debriefed and assigned. Plus, we needed several hundred telephones with multiple lines and computers and office equipment. And we needed to eat—the space had to have a place to feed us, and somewhere for us to catch up on sleep.

All this had to happen quickly. The body bags were piling up at an unacceptable rate. We had no time to plan, design, and build the space. And forget about government procurement rules, which slowed the process considerably—we needed a space now.

As luck would have it, there was a multistory office building next to police headquarters with several floors vacant. This required a large amount of money, and that is where the FBI and their allied federal agencies excel. Compared to our own extremely limited state resources, and equally limited county resources, the feds had an open wallet. They funded the office space.

While the new space was being equipped, the intelligence group was moved out of police headquarters to the Montgomery County Police Training Academy several miles away. We were thankful to get out of the din that headquarters had become. At the academy, we had space. We set up in a large classroom and got ourselves organized.

After seventeen hours, I headed home about 10 p.m. At that moment I just wanted to get home, hug my wife, hug my daughter, and make sure my grown stepsons were okay. Then I wanted a shower and several hours of sleep. This wasn't going to be a sprint to the finish. This was going to be a marathon. I just prayed the police would win in the end. Growing up watching shows like *Adam 12*, *The FBI*, and *Walker, Texas Ranger*, I had come to expect the good guys to win at the end of every show. So we had to win. We weren't going to stop until the bad guys had been run to ground.

12

October 5, 5:30 a.m. It felt like my head had just hit the pillow when suddenly my alarm was buzzing. Not sure if I was waking from a bad dream, I rolled over and looked at the clock; it was blinking 5:30 a.m. Just over four hours of sleep. At first, I stared at the date on the clock—Saturday, the fifth. Saturday was supposed to be my day off. Why the hell was my alarm going off? We had family plans, but what were they? Whatever they were, they sure as hell didn't involve getting up at 5:30 a.m. Jean wouldn't have scheduled anything this damn early.

In time, the fog in my brain started to dissipate, and I remembered. I was to be at the Montgomery County Training Academy by 7 a.m. for a meeting with Captain McAndrew and Detective Sergeant Cornwell. We were assembling our intelligence and investigative team for the sniper case.

I was physically and mentally tired, but this was just the beginning. I dragged myself out of bed and headed for a quick shower. As I passed the TV, I clicked on the news, keeping the volume low so it wouldn't wake Jean. Thankfully, there was nothing on the news that I didn't already know about. By the time I got out of the shower and had dressed, Jean was up.

I never realized how much my job affected my wife until after I had retired and was able to talk to her about some of the things I had done during my career. She knew there were things that I wasn't allowed to tell her. She also knew there were things that I wouldn't tell her. She never pressed me for information. Because I valued the devotion, trust, and love we have, I wasn't about to let what I did for a living come between us, as it had for so many troopers.

This case, however, was different. This case bothered me like no other case ever had, to my very core. I had seen people in unimaginable conditions—beaten severely, dead, decomposed. I had seen people whose heads had been blown off. I had interviewed women and children who had been brutally raped. I had seen just about every brutality that man can dish out to other human beings. I had interviewed killers and molesters, digging deep for the resolve needed to make them at ease enough with me to confess their crimes or just to tell me what had happened to them. In one case, I had to listen without reaction to one killer describe how much he enjoyed smashing a ten-year-old's naked body and head into a concrete dugout wall at a local baseball field. To get the confession, I had to let him think that I fantasized about doing the same thing. I had to let him think that I secretly admired him.

I had pulled dead men, women, and children out of smashed cars. I had held hands with dying, drunken teenagers as they drew their last breath, just so they weren't alone when they passed. I had held together the sliced-open head of a teenager until our state police helicopter could take her to the trauma center. Then I had to hug her mother, holding her hand, my uniform still covered in her daughter's blood. None of that had ever bothered me like this case did.

Maybe it was because my teenage daughter lay just a few steps away, asleep in her room, maybe dreaming about cheerleading or having fun with her friends. Maybe it was knowing I couldn't protect her from these predators lurking out there, waiting to strike again. I was torn between that type-A macho trooper supercop image that I had of myself and the reality of being a dad. How could I look at danger with defiance? How could I have a clue about how to protect my family—*any* family—from these scumbags when law enforcement from two states and the FBI didn't know who they were or where they were?

Common sense told me the chance of these killers targeting my kid or my stepsons was remote. But the dad side of me was starting to fear it. What if they were outside my daughter's school? What if they were across the parking lot or street from a gas station that Jean or one of the boys happened to stop at to get gas or a snack? I couldn't be everywhere—as a cop, I knew that. Nor could I hit the street looking for the snipers while at the same time stay home and protect my family. Fear versus reality.

I shuddered. Mentally, I locked the fear away, then I strapped on my sidearm and checked: loaded with a full magazine and one in the chamber. I slipped my badge over my neck, the metal chain cold on my skin. Ready to go.

I kissed Jean goodbye. "I'm not sure when I'll be home. Just keep Samantha home or inside. Don't let her run around at the mall or anywhere in public with her friends."

"Here's your lunch," Jean said. "And here's something for the road." She handed me a Pop Tart. Cop comfort food. *God, I love this woman*, I thought. *She knows more about me than I do about myself.*

I headed for the cruiser in the driveway. Before I got in, I took a deep breath of fresh air. The hunt for the Beltway snipers was on, in earnest. Today's game plan: to turn from the hunted into the hunters.

At the academy, I was shown to a large classroom. This was the place we would call home until the joint operations center was up and running. The immediate problem was our location. We were separated from the focal point of the investigation, which was Montgomery County police headquarters. General communications would be an issue, not to mention keeping up with breaking leads. But we needed this space. We were just going to have to work through the communications issues for the time being.

The team was beginning to file in. I knew the analysts from my own agency and had briefly met the analysts from Montgomery County. A pair of analysts from the FBI and two or three analysts from ATF joined the team. After quick introductions, we began to settle in and take stock of what we had to work with. Next door there was a computer lab where Rapid Start had been deployed, and information from tip calls was already beginning to be loaded live. A backlog of tips had been gathered in several cardboard boxes and brought over to us from headquarters. We would have to load those into the system.

There was a quick learning and training session to familiarize us with Rapid Start. A normal formal training session for the program was about sixteen hours. We had about sixteen minutes. Sixteen hours was a luxury we couldn't afford, when people were being murdered on a regular and random basis.

Each classroom had been equipped with at least two televisions tuned to local stations, Fox, and CNN. As much as I was beginning to loathe the media and the around-the-clock coverage of this case, while we were offsite at the academy classroom it was our best source of investigative information. As the case progressed, we had gotten used to hearing new information on the networks before getting any word from headquarters.

Still, we had Captain McAndrew as our liaison between

headquarters and the academy. He was in charge of relaying information, bringing back new lead and tip sheets, and keeping us in the loop with the lead investigative team until we could all get over to the joint operations center.

After our crash course in Rapid Start, several of the analysts started entering leads into the system. The rest of us sat down in the classroom in front of a whiteboard. Time to figure out where to begin the hunt.

In the modern world, everybody leaves an electronic footprint. It's now almost impossible to go completely off the grid. There are thousands of cameras everywhere, from store and parking lots to traffic cameras and ATM machines. There are license plate readers. And of course everyone uses credit cards, debit cards, commuter easy pass cards. Records are kept by every business on nearly every activity in our day. We were determined to take advantage of those records. Somewhere out there, the killers were leaving electronic bread crumbs. It was our job to look for them.

But where do we begin tracking the snipers in cyber world? We compiled a list. The obvious starting place: owners of white vans and white box trucks in three states. Stolen vehicle lists were something else we should look at; in fact we needed to recheck them at least twice a day. We also wanted to look at registered gun owners who had registered a .223-caliber weapon. We all knew that most criminals don't register their weapons, and oftentimes the weapons they use are stolen. But we would have been remiss not to look. We needed to compile a list of all known felons in the same tristate region and D.C., and to collect VICAP (Violent Criminal Apprehension Program, a database run by the FBI) data and compare it to our growing list of data sets. We would look at all the sign-in lists at shooting ranges around the region.

We spent the entire weekend of October 5 and 6 brainstorming about where the snipers may have left tracks, and how to find those tracks. What about Michaels craft stores? Could the shooters be disgruntled present or former employees? Could they be connected to a contract that went bad, and the shootings in and around the stores were a sick effort to scare away customers? We were casting a very large net over two or three states and D.C. The trick was going to be casting a large enough net, but one that wasn't so unreasonably large that the single footprint or lead would get lost among all the data collected. We had no other, easier alternative. The details were going to matter greatly.

By Sunday we were hopeful that the snipers had taken the weekend off, but we suspected the killing was going to continue. In fact, a part of us worried that the shootings would just stop cold and the killers would vanish. As perverse as it sounded, we almost *needed* more shootings in order to get more evidence and more clues so we could have a chance to catch the bastards. So far, we hadn't slowed the killers at all. As the uniform presence and pressure increased, they had simply adapted and moved their killing zone farther south into the District and now Northern Virginia. All we could do was add more cops and spread the search over a larger area. As a task force, we were maxed out on uniformed cops. We were trying to plug leaks in the dam with as many fingers as we had. But with every shooting and every killing, the dam sprang more leaks.

There were now more than six hundred investigators assigned to the case, with additional federal resources on the way. We had between eight hundred and a thousand uniformed officers, troopers, and deputies on the street, all of them not only tending to their normal responsibilities, but also actively looking for the snipers. With our initial list of data sets complete, we sent the troopers assigned to the intelligence group out into the field to retrieve the data. Our next problem would be parsing that data when it came in. Information was likely going to come to us stored on access databases, spreadsheets, handwritten logs, and any number of software packages. Some info would be sent on CDs, some via e-mail data dumps. It was going to be a job just to get it all into a common format.

When it came to the technology involved in collecting all this data, most of us, including me, were ill prepared. I knew what I needed a computer to do, but I had no idea how to make that happen. The FBI gave us funding to purchase off-the-shelf servers and computer equipment. But we still needed expertise to make all this data work together. And we needed technology. Even if we knew how to do it manually, which we didn't, too many civilians were paying with their lives for us to piss around trying to do this by hand.

13

During my narcotics investigation days, I used a program called Case Explorer to conduct link analysis. It helped us track street dealers and link them back to their supply source. Narcotics officers and troopers would enter everything they had—drug tips, information about everybody they arrested, known associates of the people arrested, and places they frequented. The program would link this information together, helping law enforcement get a clearer picture faster.

At the moment, however, the Case Explorer program was undergoing further development to make it more comprehensive— to be able to receive drug data from local, city, county, state, and federal agencies. The people working on it were at the Baltimore/ Washington High Intensity Drug Trafficking Area (HIDTA), and we weren't sure if Case Explorer was available or, if it was, if it would even help.

Captain McAndrew called Lieutenant Colonel Tom Carr, HIDTA director and a former Maryland state trooper, and Carr agreed to dedicate his staff to helping us with this sniper case. The bad news was that the new, improved Case Explorer program wasn't ready to be rolled out. But right away—that very week-end—Carr sent us three young programmers, along with the program as it then existed. He said his programmers thought they could modify Case Explorer to suit our needs.

Within five minutes of arrival, these guys got to work. On top of modifying Case Explorer to do what we needed it to do, they were rewriting code for Rapid Start so the programs could talk to each other and share information. As the data sets were brought into our intelligence section in various formats, these programmers worked nonstop to convert that data to a format that would work with Case Explorer. It was a monumental task, and these young tech guys tackled it head-on. Over the next three weeks I would see them scratch their heads, cuss, and slam their laptops shut numerous times. But they never quit. And they never said that anything we requested of them could not be done.

While the programmers worked, our investigation went into overdrive. Over that first weekend, our intelligence group began round-the-clock operation. I was assigned the day shift, and Detective Sergeant Cornwell was assigned the night shift. It was supposed to be twelve-hour shifts, but in order to make sure we stayed on the same page, it was more like eighteen-hour shifts. That same weekend, the press conferences increased in frequency. Chief Moose was now out in front of the press twice a day. The case was now receiving twenty-four-hour coverage on all the cable news channels. Every news conference was being broadcast live as breaking news on all the network and local TV channels. Any number of experts were being paraded in front of TV cameras to offer their opinions on who the snipers were and what their motivation was behind the killings. These included former homicide detectives from Los Angeles and New York; former FBI agents; and former retired military colonels and generals, all offering their expert opinion. The consensus among the talking heads was that this was obviously some sort of terrorist plot aimed at hindering the United States government. *Well, holy shit,* I thought. *What the hell am I doing here if these guys have it all figured out from New York or wherever the hell they were broadcasting from?*

The comments were irritating when they weren't totally laughable. One of the common threads from these experts was that it was important *never* to discuss police tactics via public media, because the perpetrators might be listening. Then right after spewing their disclaimer, they would discuss in detail what the police were doing and the investigative techniques that were probably being employed or that *should be* employed—in their expert opinion.

The other clear message being regurgitated among the media was that the FBI needed to step in and take complete control of the investigation. The "local agencies" weren't capable of handling the case, the press said. Yet the FBI had made it perfectly clear that the primary responsibility for the investigation rested with the Montgomery County Police Department, and that the FBI was there, as a committed partner, at the request of Montgomery County. Since the case had crossed state lines, the FBI would have been within their authority to take over the investigation, but they had chosen not to do so, which we greatly appreciated. I think they didn't want to jeopardize the close relationship that these local, city, county, state, and federal law enforcement agencies had with one another—a closeness that had come about during the attack on the Pentagon the year before. All these agencies and our intelligence officers met frequently and talked on a weekly basis. There was already a great deal of trust among us.

The federal government has a lot of rules and protocols that have to be followed in order to free up funding for a massive investigation like this. One of those protocols was to name the investigation and task force, which is how we became the SNIPMUR task force—short for "sniper murders." Unfortunately, the word SNIPMUR makes the person saying it sound like he has a terrible lisp. The name did result in considerable dark cop humor, but none of us really cared what they called us, as long as we got our funding. We needed the joint operations center built and fully operational.

During that same first weekend of the case, the FBI had brought in their profilers to assist us. Their best guess, based on what little bit of information we had at the time, was that we were probably looking for two or three white guys with military background or training. The FBI was also assisting with preparing for the frequent press conferences in an effort to manage the information being released and to help solicit public cooperation. During one of the press conferences that first weekend, the Maryland governor, Parris Glendening, was paraded out in front of the press at police headquarters. He was supposed to reassure the nervous public that the full resources of the state were being utilized in this investigation. But then he went off script and challenged the snipers by calling them cowards and telling them that we will protect our children.

Our intelligence group watched the news conference on one of the TVs in the classroom. We all sat there in silence as the governor called the killers cowards. I remember uttering, "Oh, shit," and I think that captured the collective response of the dozen or so of us in the room. We were stunned. Governor Glendening had unwittingly just put a bull's-eye on the forehead of every child in Maryland.

———

At 10 p.m. on Sunday, I called it a day. I was exhausted and wanted to go home and get a few hours sleep before coming back Monday morning and doing it all over again. Heading home, I thought about all we had accomplished over the weekend. We still didn't have any tangible leads, but at least now we were organized. The old adage "Plan the work, work the plan" is extremely important, especially in an investigation like this. Our plan was being implemented even as I drove toward home. Detective Sergeant Cornwell was working the night shift. His goal was to use that overnight time to get Case Explorer loaded on all our computer equipment, as well as to have his team assist the HIDTA programmers in modifying the software so it would be ready to receive our data.

That was all well and good, but as I drove I couldn't help worrying that the governor's words would come back to bite us. I'm no psychologist, but if I were the snipers and I had heard what the governor said, I would take it as a direct challenge. *Let's hope they haven't heard*, I thought. Though since the radio and TV media were rebroadcasting the governor's words nearly around the clock, there was little chance of that.

We were already in protection mode—I knew that. We had every school in Montgomery County covered, and all the schools in Maryland, Virginia, and the District of Columbia had been alerted. Now all we could do was hope that our efforts would be good enough.

The police radio was relatively quiet, and traffic was noticeably light on Interstate 270 as I headed north to Frederick County. Many of the vehicles on the road were marked Maryland State Police cruisers. I stopped several times, to back up one trooper after another, as each pulled over yet another white box truck or van.

14

Monday, October 7. Once again I was up early and on my way to Montgomery County and the academy. On this day that ought to be just another school day, my daughter's safety plagued my thoughts. I knew that, statistically, the odds of my Samantha being the kid on the wrong end of the rifle sights were very long, but still I couldn't get the fear out of my head. I suspected that every parent who had turned on a TV or radio over the past several days must be thinking and fearing the same thing.

But as a parent who had spent a career in law enforcement, I knew I had to push these thoughts to the back of my mind. More than that, I had to use them as *motivation*, just like back in my high school baseball days when a kid from another team told me before our game that he was going to hit two home runs off me. It pissed me off, so on my first pitch to him I drilled him in the back with my best fastball. And I struck him out three times during the rest of the game. *Channel the anger*, I thought. *Focus. Figure out who these bastards are and track their sorry asses down.*

I was at the academy by 6 a.m. Detective Sergeant Cornwell and two of the computer geeks were bleary-eyed.

"You look like hell," I said.

Cornwell looked at me and smiled. "You don't look all that much better, and you haven't worked through the night. But good news—Case Explorer is online. We've already started entering data into the system, and a good bit of the Rapid Start data is already in there."

"Seriously?"

"In a few hours, it should all be integrated. No more double data entry. We'll just do a data dump from Rapid Start to Case Explorer every couple of hours."

"That's fantastic," I said. "I would kiss you, you ugly bastard, but I'm already married."

I looked at the analysts. They had spent the night entering all the handwritten tip sheets into Case Explorer. We already had one hell of a team.

Now to use the data to create leads.

The first order of business was to make some rules so as to prioritize the value of the information we were getting. We decided on a simple color code system. Since we had nothing in the form of solid information beyond the white box truck or white van, we couldn't afford to ignore anything. Any bit of information might be the missing puzzle piece that would break the case. So we assigned colors to each lead. A green lead would be a low-priority lead. It would be a tip or a bit of information that currently didn't match any other information that was known, like tips from people who thought their ex-husbands or their neighbors or bosses were responsible. Usually, their rationale was that they thought the person was capable of committing such a crime. Still, those tips and leads would be placed in a green jacket and set aside for the time being.

The next category was a yellow lead. This lead possibly came from two or more sources, or there could be something else that might raise a few eyebrows. Examples: tips turned in from more than one source about the same person, or the tip that came in about the ex-husband wife's boyfriend who has talked about killing people or was a member of a motorcycle gang. These would be placed in a yellow jacket and would be set aside and worked up when the time permitted.

Red leads were the highest-priority leads. These were leads that came in based on tips, information, and Case Explorer database matches. If the registered owner of a white van or white box truck was also a registered owner or was known to be in possession of a .223-caliber rifle, they would be considered a higher priority. The more data sets that matched, the higher the priority assigned to the lead. A registered owner of a white van with a felony record who was a known gang member, was identified as a suspect in VICAP, or was a match to any of the data would be a red lead.

For red leads, our group would do as complete a background check as we could from the available data. This would include driving record, criminal record, known vehicle, known registered weapons, last known address, place of last employment, and any other available information. All of it would be placed in a red folder. Red folders would be turned over to an investigative team. The field investigators would be assigned these leads and would take the information into the field with them. Depending on the lead itself, they would act in what they believed was in the best interest of furthering the lead: either eliminate the person or persons as suspects, or develop the lead further. Their follow-up could include interviews of neighbors, employers, even the person named. Or if the lead was deemed serious or promising enough, the person might be placed under surveillance.

By the time our full complement of analysts had arrived, we were beginning to crank out leads, with the higher priority leads getting the full work-up. With a group of eight to ten analysts and three or four plainclothes troopers, the Intelligence Division was a hub of activity. Everyone was fully engaged in the team effort. The room was awash in chatter. TVs were on, and the usual talking heads were on various news networks giving opinions on the snipers, the challenges to finding them, and what it all meant. Team members were bantering, sharing information, and singling out tips for follow up.

Since the weekend, I had been in contact with my friend and colleague Lieutenant Tom Chase, criminal investigation commander for Frederick City. Tom and I had worked on many of the same cases over the years and had become close friends. This particular morning, I was briefing him on the ongoing investigation. Briefing reports had been going out to all the allied agencies on a daily basis, but by the time it was received by the agencies, the information was usually at least twenty-four hours old. There was more updated news coming from the network and cable news channels.

I knew Tom would pass that information on not just to his own agency, but also to the Frederick County sheriff's department and the two smaller police departments in the county. We talked about the theory that this was somehow connected to Michaels craft stores, and Tom said the Frederick City police and the sheriff's department were trying to keep a close watch on those parking lots.

Then I brought up my thinking on where the snipers were laying their heads. Tom and I agreed: they would not sleep where they killed. Since all the killings had occurred in Montgomery County and were now moving south into Northern Virginia, I had a hunch they were located north, which would make Frederick a logical location. Or maybe they were somewhere northeast, perhaps Baltimore. Tom concurred.

My rationale for calling and briefing Tom was twofold. I wanted to give him this information on a professional basis, but I also hoped that sharing info with him might help protect my wife and kids. Jean worked in Frederick, and my daughter went to school there. It was where we lived. It might be just a matter of time before the snipers targeted a kid, and I didn't want it to be mine.

Turns out it wasn't. Sometime before 8:30 that morning, my cell phone rang. It was Captain McAndrew with the news we had feared: At 8:08 a.m., there was a shooting at Benjamin Tasker Middle School, located in Bowie, Prince George's County. Iran Brown, a thirteen-year-old student, was shot as he got out of his mother's car in front of the school.

I slammed my fist on the desk. I wanted to cry—we *knew* this would happen. I could feel the hot wave of anger overtaking me. "Goddamn it!" I shouted, to the room in general. "Those fuckers heard the stupid fucking comment the governor made and took him up on it! This bullshit has got to be stopped!"

No sooner had I hung up with the captain and told the group what had happened than it appeared on our TV screen, with live coverage from the scene. We watched in silence. All of us figured that the snipers had been listening to everything the media said, and were no doubt getting off on it. Meanwhile, we were doing our best, thinking they would attack where they had already struck. Instead, they moved one county east and south, away from where our troopers were waiting for them. They were playing us.

My emotions were jumbled—I was heartbroken that this had happened to that family, but I was thankful that it wasn't *my* family. Such thoughts were new to me—in all my years of law enforcement, I had been able to put personal concerns aside. But this case was under my skin. I knew that many of us in that room were feeling the same thing, but I had to tamp down my feelings. None of the team needed to see that the person in charge was letting the chaos get to him. Looking around the room, I could see anger on every face. No doubt part of it was that we didn't have the information and the data we needed. Our upset cemented our resolve, but resolve alone wasn't going to solve this case.

We alerted the Prince George's County school district and police department. But beyond keeping kids inside and increasing the frequency of regular patrols and the presence of school resource police officers, there was nothing more we could do. We simply couldn't be everywhere. The small piece of good news: Iran was alive and would ultimately recover from his wounds.

As it turned out, law enforcement had learned about this shooting the same way the rest of the country had: via television. It was an ongoing problem during the course of the investigation. Part of the reason for this lack of information flow was the simple dynamics and massive size of this investigation. Every day, more police agencies were involved, along with more local police officers and federal agents that had been shipped in from all over the country. The investigation had quickly become unwieldy. It was impossible to get vital information in a timely manner to the people who needed it. As resources poured in, this problem would grow (it was never completely solved). There is a need to share, but there was also an element of need to know. It's a decision that must be made on every case. For a localized case, it's easy: those people were the lead investigator, the prosecutor, and investigative team leaders and supervisors. In a case like this it was much harder to manage.

So was disseminating information that wasn't considered primary. Again, with this shooting, witnesses at the scene and in the area of the school all reported seeing a white van cruising the area and stopping near the school. This sighting was again repeated by the media.

If there was anything positive about this, it was fact that when it comes to any criminal investigation, even negatives can be a positive. The teams that were out there conducting surveillance on suspects could now deem some of them cleared of suspicion. If they were under surveillance when Iran was shot, clearly they couldn't be responsible. So we could stop expending our resources following them around.

If there hadn't been a media frenzy and public panic before Iran was shot, there sure were now. It's bad enough when adults are shot; it's another level of fear and helplessness when the victim is a child. The public outcry was suddenly into the stratosphere. That meant the pressure on all law enforcement was excruciating. Everyone involved with this investigation felt it.

15

Investigators flooded the area around the school and sealed it off. It was quickly determined that the shot had come from a wooded area across the street. A careful, systematic search found tangible evidence: shoe prints in the dirt at the spot where the shooter was thought to have stood. Also at the scene, lying backside up among the leaves, was what appeared to be a playing card bearing a handwritten message: "For you Mr. Police, call me God, do not release to the press." Once the card was turned over, it was evident that it was a Death tarot card. On the face side, handwritten above the death-head emblem, were the words "Call me God." The block print messages were simply written, like something you might see scrawled on the wall of a public restroom stall.

The discovery of this physical evidence was not shared with us in the intelligence section. In fact, most of the thousand-plus police officers working on this case were kept in the dark about it. Only those at the scene and a select group of the task force leadership were aware of the discovery, which made total sense: law enforcement needed time to consider what it meant.

Several things were now clear, though. This tiny bit of communication told us that we were dealing with an organized, well-planned act of terrorism. The killers were responding to the governor's direct challenge from the day before, conveyed to them by the press. This proved that they were listening, and probably enjoying their anonymous fame. The "call me God" message indicated that the snipers—if there was indeed more than one, which seemed to be the case—now had a god complex; they felt like they were in complete control.

Maybe there would be ways to use this to our advantage, but first we had to quell the growing panic. If news of the evidence got out before we were prepared to deal with it, we would have a public state of emergency on our hands. Not that we weren't already close to that. With the shooting of Iran Brown, schools were canceled in Northern Virginia, and Maryland canceled fall sports programs across the state, including football. The fear was palpable.

That afternoon we were advised that, as of the following morning, our intelligence operation would be based in the joint operations center—the JOC—across from Montgomery County Police headquarters. Finally we would be in the same building, and on the same floor, with the rest of the investigative team. This would dramatically increase our ability to stay current on the case, plus

The first shot fired in the Beltway sniper case. On October 2, 2002, a bullet pierced the glass of a Michaels craft store window in Aspen Hill, Maryland. The bullet was intended for the cashier but missed its mark. It was initially thought to be a random act of vandalism.

October 2, early evening. Montgomery County police respond to the homicide of James Martin, who was gunned down while loading groceries into his car in front of a Shoppers Food Warehouse on Georgia Avenue in Wheaton, Maryland.

October 3, 7:41 a.m. James Buchanan is shot while mowing grass in front of a car dealership in Rockville, Maryland.

After being struck by the bullet that cost him his life, Buchanan staggered back onto the lot, where he collapsed. A fellow employee found him a few feet from the mower. Initially it was thought his injuries were from a freak accident involving the lawn mower.

October 3, 8:12 a.m. Premkumar Walekar was shot while he pumped gas into his taxi at a Mobil gas station in Aspen Hill, only a few minutes' drive from where Buchanan had been shot.

This crime scene photo demonstrates the blood splatter caused by the high-speed bullet that struck Walekar. He was killed because he was in the wrong place at the wrong time and was a target of opportunity.

Crime scene photo of the Crisp & Juicy restaurant in Silver Spring, Maryland, where Sarah Ramos was shot at 8:37 a.m. while she sat on a bench waiting for a bus. All three murders were committed in a very short period and within a few miles of each other.

Ramos's shooting was initially reported as a suicide, but Montgomery County police quickly realized she was shot with a high-speed bullet fired from a distance. This photo shows the approximate location from where the bullet was thought to have been fired. Witnesses reported seeing a white box truck or van leaving the area immediately after the shooting.

Crime scene photo of Lori Ann Lewis-Rivera's van. She was shot at 9:58 a.m. as she vacuumed her minivan at a Shell gas station less than two miles from the Crisp & Juicy restaurant. She was killed while Montgomery County police were working the other crime scenes amid heavy police presence in the area.

By the afternoon of October 4, the second day, forensics has determined the victims had been shot with a .223-caliber rifle, most likely a Bushmaster. The author is holding the Bushmaster sniper rifle, now in possession of the National Law Enforcement Museum.

Crime scene photo of the corner in the District of Columbia, just across the Maryland state line, where Pascal Charlot was shot and killed as he walked down the street at 9:30 p.m. on October 3.

Crime scene photo of the sniper nest from where the bullet that killed Charlot was fired. It was located across the street from where he fell.

Crime scene photo of the parking lot of the Michaels craft store in the Spotsylvania Mall in Fredericksburg, Virginia, thirty-five miles south of Washington, D.C., where Caroline Seawell was shot in the back at 2:30 p.m., October 4.

Crime scene photo of the front of the Benjamin Tasker Middle School, Bowie, Prince Georges County, Maryland, where Iran Brown was shot on October 7 at 8:08 a.m. as he got out of his mother's car. The shot came from a wooded area across the street from the school entrance.

ABOVE Crime scene photo of the first communication from the snipers in the form of a death-head tarot card found in the woods where the shot that struck Iran Brown came from.

RIGHT Flip side of the death-head tarot card. The snipers wrote "Call me God" in the top margin.

Crime scene photo from October 9, when at 8:18 p.m. Dean
Myers was shot as he pumped gas into his car at a Sunoco station
in Manassas, Virginia, just off Interstate 95.

Crime scene photo from October 11 of an Exxon station just off I-95 in Fredericksburg, Virginia. At 9:30 a.m. Kenneth Bridges was gunned down as he put gas into his car. The shot was heard by a Virginia state trooper who was working an accident on the interstate just a few hundred yards from the Exxon station.

Crime scene photo of the press gathering at the scene where Bridges was shot. By this time there was a press frenzy surrounding the investigation.

it would help us share new information and tips with the investigators in a more timely manner. This investigation was growing bigger and more complex with every hour. From a communications and information perspective, we were behind the curve and struggling to keep up. Getting everybody together in the same building was going to be a big help.

By midafternoon, a clearly shaken Chief Moose took to the podium in front of Montgomery County headquarters for a press conference. Televised live by every cable news channel and major TV network in the country, as well as news agencies from around the world, Chief Moose sought to accomplish two goals: one, to calm an increasingly nervous and upset public; and two, to try to draw out the murderers and encourage direct contact with them. Looking haggard from exhaustion, the chief stared right into the cameras and spoke directly to the snipers.

"Shooting a kid: I guess it's getting really personal now."

The FBI's Gary Bald, special agent in charge of the bureau's Baltimore field office, also addressed the press. Special Agent Bald was now the lead federal agent in charge of federal resources assigned to the investigation. He and Chief Moose fielded multiple questions from the assembled press corps. Bald was asked if the FBI had taken over the case, and were they now in charge. Was this a terrorist attack? Was this a new way for the terrorists responsible for September 11 to attack the United States of America? What was the FBI going to do about this?

To his credit, Bald was able to address all these issues. He made sure to indicate that the primary responsibility for this investigation still rested with the Montgomery County Police Department and the local agencies in both Virginia and the District of Columbia. He stressed that the SNIPMUR task force was a joint venture, and the cooperation between local, city, state, and federal agencies was unprecedented and would lead to the ultimate apprehension of those responsible for these killings and shootings. With live press conferences happening at least twice a day, this case was virtually being investigated in front of a captivated TV audience.

———

That evening, we began moving the intelligence section to the JOC. Our operation stopped just long enough to get our people over to the new location. The night shift reported to the JOC, and the lead-producing machine, along with the background check function, did not stop. We were housed with the field investigative team in a large open office space called the bullpen, which covered the entire third floor of the building.

The room looked like a construction project gone bad. The drop ceiling had just a few of the panels still in place. Miles of telephone cables and computer cables had been run above the ceiling's metal grid system. Desks were grouped together in clumps of four to six, and cables hung loosely from the ceiling, providing multiple telephone lines and power to the desktop computers. None of the furniture matched. It had all been dragged in from some federal warehouse somewhere. Chairs behind the desks were a variety of fold-up chairs and a few desk chairs with wheels that had seen better days. I remember looking at Cornwell and saying "Hey, now we're right at home. Just like any state police barrack around the state—all old and nothing matches, but it's serviceable."

"Yeah," he said, with a tired smile. "You can sit on one of these old office chairs and get poked in the ass and rip your pants on a spring sticking up out of the seat. Just like home."

We had divided the room into work areas for the various functions that were being performed. Our section, occupying a large corner of the room, was our think tank. Beside us was a call center where tips and other information came in. Another large area was dedicated to the field investigators, who came and went like worker bees in a hive. There was also an area dedicated to assigning the leads to field investigators. People working that area were also responsible for receiving and reviewing the filed reports that resulted from the agents conducting interviews and surveillances. All of this meant that everyone in the room was now privy to twists and turns in the investigation as they happened, as opposed to hearing about them a day later—or not at all. We were now fast-tracked into becoming the cohesive team that we needed to be if we were going to pursue these killers to the ends of the earth.

The command center included several break-out conference rooms equipped with maps, charts, workflow charts, and pictures of the victims and crime scenes. Another section was dedicated to the FBI profilers and the public relations people, who not only orchestrated the press conferences but also answered the avalanche of media questions and requests for updates and interviews. Captain Forsyth and the lead investigative team from Montgomery County occupied offices that lined one of the walls. Space was utilized as is, with little or no modifications other than the running of the miles of cables that were required to make this a functional joint operations center.

A separate room, walled off in glass, contained the growing number of computer servers that had been brought in for the investigation—along with a large number of tech staff to keep the systems up and running. Our servers containing Case Explorer and its revisions were also linked to this data center. And in order to keep us humans functioning, a hallway became a makeshift cafeteria. With more than a thousand officers and investigators working 24/7, there was a constant need for food (catered), snacks, fruit, coffee (gallons), and water.

The acquiring of the space and the building out and outfitting of the joint operations center had been accomplished in just over forty-eight hours. Given the daunting logistics of an operation of this magnitude, it was amazing that a center could be readied and put into operation in such a short time. The mismatched furniture, the cables, the computers, and the work stations appeared nearly overnight, as if by magic—thanks not to Santa's elves but to Uncle Sam's.

Security also mattered, and the center's security became the responsibility of the U.S. Marshals Service and Federal Protective Service. It's a job they took very seriously—our security was nearly as tight as it is around a sitting president. Everyone assigned to work in the JOC had a picture badge that included his or her name, the name of the investigation and the joint operations center, and the name of the person's home agency. The badge had to be worn at all times while in the center; entrance was denied without it. In a small corridor where the elevator opened, credentials were immediately checked. No one, especially the press, could leave the elevator unless he or she had been issued a badge.

With all the cops and all the guns present 24/7, our physical security was the easy part. Not so simple was operational security—keeping a lid on info that we didn't want the public to know for investigative reasons. This was the real security problem, and it was never resolved fully. With so many conversations going on in this command center, we seasoned investigators were constantly worried that something said here would somehow leak beyond our fortified walls, and sink the ship.

16

October 8, 2002. As Monday evening turned into Tuesday morning, we barely noticed that a new day had begun. We were in the thick of the job, carrying out our assigned duties. Meanwhile, several big-screen televisions were mounted on one of the walls of the JOC, all of them tuned to cable news channels except one, which was set to a local Washington station, Channel 9. That morning a segment on Channel 9 reported on the death-head tarot card that investigators had found in the woods at Benjamin Tasker Middle School. The reporter described word for word what was written on the card, including the note in the hand of one of the snipers saying that we were not to release anything about the card to the press.

Everyone in the room stopped what we were doing. Stopped cold. The only sounds were the hum of the computers and the reporter on television. None of us on the intelligence staff, including Captain McAndrew, knew about this evidence. Neither, it turned out, did most, if not all, of the people in that room. Yet there it was being broadcast for the entire region to hear, including the snipers—who, we had just learned, had specifically directed the police not to release that information. We all stood there gawking at the TV in disbelief. Then the implications of what had just occurred started to set in. More than one investigator slammed files down on the tops of desks, and I heard chairs being kicked, and a cascade of swearing began to fill the room. I looked over at the glass partition that was Captain Forsyth's office. His reaction was inescapable—his face was flushed. I could see anger swelling, even from across the command center. Suddenly, he flung his chair across the room, slammed his office door, and stormed out of the JOC.

Where he was going wasn't obvious. But what *was* obvious—to him, to all of us—was that there had been a leak by somebody at the crime scene on Monday. Who leaked it? Was the leaker intentionally trying to piss off the killers? Or was this somebody looking to become a future talking head on TV, leaking evidence and facts for personal gain?

We had put together a great team of police officers and federal agents from across all jurisdictional lines. This team was now being undermined by somebody who wanted to be seen by the press as the inside source. This leak could easily spark trust issues among local, state, and federal law enforcement. "Dan," I said to Cornwell, "if I knew who the rotten bastard was that's leaking this shit I would personally kick his ass." I'm sure I wasn't alone in that sentiment.

There is always public interest in crime and police investigations, and the press serves a vital purpose to law enforcement, helping us get important information about suspects, and what to look out for, out to the public and possibly generate valuable leads. So we do what we can to work hand in hand with them. A good police reporter understands the need for police to keep certain details about an investigation out of the public eye, even as he or she works to get the story. But the problem with a case like this— one that captures national and world interest—is that it brings out the competitive nature of the news business. All the cable news networks and local stations want to scoop their competitors. Thus, responsible journalism takes a back seat to sensationalism. That's one side of it. The other side is that the same heat—that very intense national and world interest—can sometimes cause a cop to succumb to the lure of possible fame and fortune.

No matter how it happens, it's not helpful to any investigation, let alone one of this magnitude, to have to conduct it in full view of a mesmerized cable TV audience. The killers, who had yet to be identified, could track our every move; they would see us coming ten miles away. All these leaks were going to do was get more people killed.

I remember, during the course of this investigation, being in a closed conference room with about a dozen other people, all law enforcement, in which critical information and strategy concerning the case were being discussed. Ideas, investigative plans, and the course of the investigation from that particular point forward were all being hashed out. Then, within five minutes of that meeting breaking up, the details were being regurgitated damn near word for word on two of the major cable news networks.

In all my years of law enforcement experience, I had never seen anything like this. I looked at Cornwell, who was staring in disbelief at the talking head on TV. "The bastards have to be listening, Dan," I said. "The people in that room couldn't have had *time* to drop a dime and repeat the conversation. It's on TV, and I just walked out of that meeting." The media had to be pointing microphones at the windows and picking up the conversations. And they had to know that that briefing was going to happen—and where and when. "Dan, we got a damn rat in here," I said.

"It has to be a fed," Dan said. "Who the hell else could it be?"

Eventually the press leaks became so bad that everyone entering or leaving the operations center was screened, almost daily, for any planted bugs or microphones. White-noise machines were installed along all the windows in an effort to stop information from being picked up by powerful microphones pointed at the building. Reporters and news networks were hungry for fresh details. They had taken up a 24/7 encampment in the press area and around police headquarters and the operations center, and some of them would go to any length to get the scoop.

The shooting of thirteen-year-old Iran Brown had drawn the attention of President George W. Bush. During a White House press briefing, the president said he thought the snipers were people with sick minds who were getting off on terrorizing people. The White House was now being briefed daily about the progress of the investigation. This was a whole new stressor added to all of us working the case.

The gravity of the situation was now evident: People were not out and about, except to go to work. News broadcasts showed area gas stations covering their pump areas with large blue tarps in an effort to block the clear view of snipers who might want to shoot their customers. The few people who ventured out were ducking low behind their cars while fueling. People parked their cars as close as possible to their destination, then hurried into stores and buildings running in a zigzag pattern. Stores and businesses closed blinds or taped brown paper over storefront windows to prevent anyone on the outside from being able to see in. The nation's capital, and the areas around it, had started to resemble a deserted war zone.

This was not the America I had grown up in, and I felt somehow responsible for the change. In my head, it was on me as a member of law enforcement to put a stop to this. It was an irrational thought—I was just another cop on a team, and it would take a team to stop the snipers. Still, the thought was there. As the sun set on Tuesday, there was a definite uneasiness—even a dread—throughout the operations center. Would there be another shooting tonight? Would the tarot card being released to the press spur the snipers to seek some form of revenge? Since the words on the tarot card indicated the killers had a god complex, it was a likely scenario. There were times when I wondered, *Does the press care how many innocent people got killed? Is there a bloodlust on the part of the press?* It was hard not to see them as part of a vicious, self-serving cycle: the more people who were shot, the more sensational the story; the more sensational the story, the more so-called experts they could put on TV to wildly guess what the killers were thinking and tell the public what the police should be doing about it; and the more the "experts" talked about the murders, the higher the TV ratings.

After working for more than two days straight, I badly needed a shower and some rest. Plus, I had to get the hell out of the operations center, if only for a few hours. I had to get back in touch with my reality, which meant going home and being a husband and a dad. Soon I eased car 662 out of the parking lot, past the tent city and the fortress of satellite trucks that lined the street. *Tough to turn all this off*, I thought.

I worked my way out of the immediate area and went north on I-270. The streets were quiet, and so was the interstate. There was very little traffic, other than police cars. What few remaining resources the state police had to add to the phalanx of police protection that we were trying to establish around all the schools had now been called on to help protect schools in Prince George's County. My personal morale was low. Going home for a few hours to my wife and daughter would be an energy and morale boost. At least I hoped it would. It always had been in the past. My wife and kids were my sanctuary, and I desperately needed to be with them right now.

17

October 9, 5:30 a.m. The day started out very much like the last several days had. It felt as though we had been working this case forever, but it had been only seven days. Once again, I was up early and out of the house. Traffic was very light—unusual for a Wednesday. I found myself staring intently at every white van or box truck that I passed. A number of them were sporting disabled-vehicle tags on the back. The uniformed cops were stopping the same vehicles time after time, so they had started attaching disabled-vehicle tags to the rear of the vans and trucks so other troopers or officers would know that the vehicle had already been stopped and checked.

As I headed to work, I wondered if we were spending too much time focusing on white vans and box trucks. Case Explorer had been making matches based on the data sets we had collected. The majority of the leads we had generated through the link analysis program had involved white vans or trucks—yet none of the leads we had passed on to the field investigators for follow-up had produced anything of use. Yes, we had identified a lot of people with felony records who were in violation of the law because they possessed firearms, primarily .223-caliber rifles, but that alone wasn't helping us in this particular case.

We had found several people with felony records who owned or drove white vans or trucks and were *also* members of known outlaw motorcycle clubs or other criminal enterprises; those people were under around-the-clock police surveillance. So far, though, none of that had produced anything concrete. I'd had my doubts from the start that the shootings had anything to do with outlaw motorcycle clubs. They'll go after one another, or after other groups because of a bad drug deal or a bar fight or some other perceived slight, but rarely do they harm an uninvolved passerby, unless by accident. If this had been club related, there would have been other evidence at the scene to suggest so. The same could be said for involvement of any of the known street gangs in the Capital area. After spending years on the street working undercover, we investigators had any number of confidential informants.

Not one of them was able to provide any relevant information to the state police or any other agency. We seemed to be chasing ghosts. All of this fed into the fear that this was some organized and well-financed terrorist cell—or worse, a complete off-the-grid lone wolf who was kill-for-thrill motivated. Since no overseas organization was laying claim to the shootings, they were looking more and more like the work of a lone wolf.

Informants weren't protecting anyone, not with a reward that was well into six figures. If there was useful information to be had out there, we would have heard about it. And I had checked with every one of my old informants from my narcotics days, plus new sources from the criminal intelligence side. All the experienced investigators working this case, along with just about every detective in Maryland, was doing the same thing, and there was nothing on the street to help us.

I made it to the JOC well before 7 a.m. and was briefed by a tired and haggard-looking Detective Sergeant Cornwell.

"You need to get out of here, go home and get some rest," I said.

"No, I'm good," he said, unconvincingly. Like me, he was in this case with both feet. "We got more data sets loaded onto Case Explorer," he continued. "We've collected terminated employee files from Michaels, and sign-in logs from surrounding rifle ranges. The team spent the night typing these into the system. And the coders have developed bridges that will link Case Explorer with the criminal records and DMV files from Maryland, Virginia, and D.C. They're working out the bugs, but we should be up and running on that soon."

"How's it going with Rapid Start?"

"We're online, but we're not sure if all of the tips are coming in from Virginia, since they set up their own joint command center." The frustration was evident in his voice.

"I know, but look what you've accomplished in just a few days.

Hell, what *we've* done as a team." I was trying to convince both Dan and myself. "Getting data from reluctant sources, getting other agencies to follow our protocol—that's out of our control. All we can do is voice our concerns and whine and complain to Captain McAndrew and let him try to fight those battles on our behalf. We have to stay focused on our mission."

But what if we had the wrong mission? I thought. *What if all we were doing was blowing smoke up our own asses?* I knew I couldn't think that way. But, still, the thought was there, lurking in the back of my mind.

We headed into the briefing together. The troopers and analysts from the night shift, as well as the day shift team, had assembled. I brought up the van. "We're focused on a white van, and we've gone seven days straight looking into every white van out there. But what if they're not in a white van? If not, how do we find them?" The problem, we debated, was that in every shooting, witnesses reported seeing a white van or box truck, or both, either right before or right after the shooting. We couldn't discount that. But the investigation turning up nothing at all just didn't add up.

During the morning press conference, an angry Chief Moose addressed the collected press, admonishing them over the leaked tarot card and saying that he was very sure the public didn't want Channel 9 or the *Washington Post* to lead this investigation. Beyond that, there was nothing new to tell them. We were no closer to solving this case than we had been the day this all started. Nerves were frayed, and the TV talking heads were giving the efforts of this task force a severe public beating.

We in the intelligence group kept our collective efforts focused on the job at hand. We were beginning to doubt that we would be able to contribute anything of substance to this investigation, but we had to keep trying. We had collected more than 140 data sets, ranging from small lists of people who had recently purchased .223-caliber ammunition to extremely large data sets of everyone in three states with a felony record, and that was subdivided into crimes of violence or crimes of violence in which a firearm had been used.

At 8:18 that night, I was pulling out of the parking lot when word came over the police radio: a man named Dean Myers had become the snipers' latest target when he was shot and killed as he filled his car with gasoline at a Sunoco station just off I-95 in Manassas, Virginia. Nobody heard the shot that killed Myers, but once again witnesses reported seeing a white van occupied by two men leaving the area. Just like the movie *Groundhog Day*, in which the main character wakes up every morning to repeat what had happened the day before, this was becoming the real-life nightmare that we were living in. And we couldn't seem to stop it from happening.

An all-points bulletin was issued for the white van, which was described as possibly being a Dodge Caravan. The Virginia State Police and the Prince William County sheriff's department quickly moved to secure ramps on and off I-95. Roadblocks were established quickly in an effort to try trapping the snipers. Yet none of the roadblocks or dragnets resulted in any viable suspects or additional information.

More than three hundred investigators and just as many members of the press converged on the crime scene. The Prince William County sheriff's department now joined the investigation and the task force. There is nothing that three hundred investigators at a crime scene can do other than cause additional confusion and possibly damage the crime scene. Besides, as I figured out very early in my career, the bad guys are no longer at the crime scene, so it's best to expend our energy looking for them someplace else. But I knew that this mass rush to the crime scene was as much about frustration as it was about trying to help. I also knew that the task force leadership would have to take steps to ensure there was *one* team of crime-scene investigators and evidence-collection people responding to, and in charge of, this and any future shootings.

There was nothing further I could do at the JOC that night. As much as I wanted to turn around and help with this, it wouldn't have served any purpose for me, or anybody from my team, to run to Manassas. We would only be getting in the way. We needed to stick with our mission of trying to develop leads based on the more than eight thousand tips that had come in.

But as I left the center and headed for home, I couldn't stop thinking about all those cops flooding the crime scene. We needed to be looking at this case differently. And we needed to be using all the cops on the street in a much more efficient manner.

18

October 10, 7 a.m. As the sun came up, I headed south from Frederick County to Montgomery County and the joint operations center. After another night of little sleep, I was even more convinced that the snipers were laying their heads to the north in Frederick County, or maybe northeast toward Baltimore. There hadn't been any killings or shootings in either of those directions. "Don't shit where you sleep," as the old saying goes. In my head, the snipers were avoiding committing any acts of violence where they slept. Again, trying to think like the killers—which is what I was trained to do—that's the way I would have done it.

Also, I was convinced that we were looking for the wrong vehicle. Since day one, law enforcement throughout the entire region had been stopping and searching every white van or truck, along with anything that even *remotely* looked like that type of vehicle, and we had come up with nothing. If I were the snipers and I had started out driving a white van or truck and heard all the reports that the police were focusing on this type of vehicle, I would have ditched it for something else. We knew the snipers were watching and listening to news reports about the investigation, so there was no reason to believe they didn't know we were in tunnel-vision mode looking for them in a white van or truck.

The problem was that after every shooting, including the one the night before when Dean Myers was killed, we had witnesses reporting seeing a white van. Was this because we had programmed the public into looking for white vans and that was all they noticed? It has been proven time and again that the observations of witnesses can be influenced by predisposed ideas and beliefs. The general public in the entire area was panicked. People were afraid for their children and themselves. They were getting a constant diet of information overload from every news channel or radio channel concerning this case. That was affecting everybody in the area in a personal way like no other case.

All the news channels had talked about was white vans and trucks. Pictures of white vans and trucks were plastered all over the newspapers. Before working this case, I had never noticed how many white vans and trucks are on the road. Once we all started looking, it seemed that every other damn vehicle was a white van or truck. It didn't matter if you were patrolling the interstate or cruising through the business districts, white vans and box trucks where everywhere. Was it possible that the citizens who were our witnesses were predisposed to report white vans or trucks after every shooting? I wasn't the only one thinking this way. Virginia State Police superintendent Gerald Massengill had suggested in a news conference after the Myers shooting that civilians and police should not focus *only* on white vans or trucks.

As I reported for duty that morning and received my briefing from Detective Sergeant Cornwell, I wasn't surprised that there was nothing new to report. Despite the shooting the night before, the script had just been repeated. A man was killed with a sniper's bullet, and other than the bullet matching other shootings and more sightings of a white van, there was no new evidence.

Following every shooting there was a new influx of tips and calls into the various call centers, and now those had to be vetted and entered into Rapid Start and then fed into Case Explorer. By now we had numerous people calling to confess to the crimes. These calls went immediately to the top of the list to be run down in the form of a lead. In murders that get a lot of public attention, there is usually at least one person who calls to confess, and while we do go through the tedious process of eliminating the person as a suspect, in most of these cases the tip could be discounted easily because the confessor simply didn't have enough credible information to describe the crime. But the sniper case was off the charts. Nothing could be immediately dismissed. Since we didn't have much evidence to point us in any direction, *everything* had to be given high priority—the callers saying that God had come to them in the night and told them who the shooters were, the callers fingering someone in their lives they didn't like, the clairvoyants describing exactly what the killers looked like.

All of this, like the majority of tip calls, were what I call *noise*. The higher the case profile, the more noise that is generated. In the sniper case, it felt like we were sitting in a Ford Pinto with all the windows closed, and concert-quality speakers were blaring incoherent white noise at us at full volume. It was overwhelming. But each of us had to fight through it, eliminate the noise, and stay focused on the mission. This was one of the few times in my career that I felt the case was out of control and the bad guys were calling all the shots while spitting in our faces, and there was nothing we could do about it except wait for them to make a recognizable mistake.

But I had a strong, strong feeling that we weren't looking in the right place or asking the right questions. Through my years of working the streets, both in and out of uniform, I learned first-hand about what we call a cop's sixth sense or cop's intuition. Most cops know when something just doesn't feel right. It may not be something they can legally act on, but they can feel it nevertheless.

My wife still gets irritated with me when it kicks in unexpectedly. We'll be out somewhere and she'll tell me to stop staring at somebody across the restaurant or in a store, or at another car stopped next to us at a traffic light. "Stop staring," she'll say. "There's nothing wrong with that guy—he's just going about his business." We laugh and move on, but that sense has kept me alive several times during my days in narcotics and working the road. I've learned to trust that little voice, the one every cop out there has. *Right now in this case*, I thought, *we need to tap into those thousands of little voices if we're going to catch these guys.*

In the operations center that morning, I sat back in one of the dirty-beige office chairs, the seat lumpy on one side. The wheels squeaked in protest, worn out from years of use. As I listened to the morning chatter among the group, it hit me. I knew how we could harness the instincts of the cops on the street. Cops see things that a regular person never sees. A good cop sees everything, and we had a shitload of good cops on the street.

Over the years, I frequently worked as a road trooper on the other end of a BOLO broadcast. During those lookouts, even though I was focused on trying to find a specific subject or vehicle, something else would suddenly catch my attention, for whatever reason: *that little voice.* What I had noticed maybe didn't fit what we were currently looking for, but I would call in the information to our police communication operator—the PCO—and ask for a records check. Usually I would ask them to run a check on a tag number, just to see whom the vehicle belonged to and if there were any warrants or lookouts associated with it. Most of the time when I called in those checks, it was simply because something about the vehicle or the person in it didn't seem right to me.

When the PCO runs that tag through Maryland vehicle records or the National Crime Information Center database to check on the registered owner and stolen vehicle reports, a permanent record of that tag and inquiry remains in the system. This is useful for many reasons. One, the record associates the inquiry with the police officer who requested the information; if the trooper becomes the victim of a crime, we can go back and see the last vehicle check the trooper ran, which might help us determine what happened. This permanent record also helps prevent police officers from abusing their power. We are supposed to run vehicle registrations for legitimate police business only, and there is a broad spectrum of reasons constituting "police business." But there are also reasons for running tags that would be considered abuses of power, such as to find out the name and address of a pretty girl or your ex-girlfriend—a severe offense that can get you fired. So the name association in this data is key: it ensures that an accurate audit of these records can be completed for every police officer who uses the system.

My thought was that such recordkeeping might just help us in the sniper case. I knew that all our cops were focused on looking for the killers in a white van or truck, but cops don't stop noticing other things as well. They continued to run records checks of other vehicles that had caught their attention. As we brainstormed in our corner of the operations center, I asked the group of analysts, police officers, and three of our HIDTA computer programmers to think about how we could use that information.

One suggestion I had was to draw a circle on a map at one mile, three miles, and five miles around each of the shooting locations. Then we could look at the records within those circles to see what anomalies came up. I wanted to know *every* tag number that had been checked by *every* cop in the area during a given time frame, which we decided would be from one hour before to one hour after each of the shootings. That meant we would start within that one-mile circle and expand out as we were able to get the information.

It was a great idea, but it presented huge logistical roadblocks. Because we would be looking in such a wide area, we would need to cull the records of two state systems and the District of Columbia. We would also need the records from the NCIC database. This meant getting the cooperation from administrators of all those systems. The job was also likely to be costly, both in man-hours and in computer programs for extracting the requested information. If we were able to obtain the info, it would come to us in several different program formats that would have to be converted to computer language readable by Case Explorer. We would then use Case Explorer to search for any common vehicle tags that came up at all of these shooting locations using the time-and-area parameters that we had set.

It all seemed like a monumental undertaking. And we couldn't just give up on the calls that were still flooding in. We had to keep that up, plus continue to review Case Explorer data being churned out daily—data that needed to be vetted and sent to the field investigators. How were we going to do all this? Where would the additional manpower come from? I didn't have answers to those questions, but I knew it was time for us to think and act outside the box.

Leave it to the geeks. The HIDTA programmers had a solution in mind. They said if they could get clean data, they could write programming into Case Explorer that would allow us to run a pattern search. This meant we could search through *all* the tags in the various police systems and come up with those tags that matched in each of the given regions using the time frame of one hour before and one hour after each of the shootings.

Suddenly there was renewed energy in the room. The analysts went back to looking through and evaluating tips and matches that Case Explorer was already producing, and Captain McAndrew set out to make sure the various database authorities would provide us with the information we needed. The technical modifications wouldn't happen overnight, and there were many problems that each of these system administrators would need to overcome, including their own security protocols. But with all the obstacles, Captain McAndrew was the right man to head the effort.

As a former Marine, McAndrew was a commander I would have followed to hell and back; I knew he would never order me to do something that he wasn't willing to do himself. Back when I was under his command, we'd had several nose-to-nose arguments about the way things should be done, and though I was able to get him to wiggle some in each of those arguments, he was the captain; he always won. Now, while it was comforting to know that he was in charge, I also knew he felt his responsibility deeply, and I could only guess the toll this case was taking on him. Not that he showed it like the rest of us. After eight days of my working nearly around the clock, my shirt and pants weren't always ironed, and my tie was loose around my neck. McAndrew looked like a Marine recruiting poster. His suit and tie always looked fresh and pressed. Detective Sergeant Cornwell, who was every bit as exhausted as I was, wondered out loud if McAndrew was spraying Scotch Guard on the inside of his suits. He never appeared to sweat.

19

October 11, 9:30 a.m. Kenneth Bridges was pumping gas into his car at an Exxon station just off I-95 in Fredericksburg when he was struck and killed by a sniper's bullet. Just a few hundred yards away, a uniformed Virginia state trooper was working an accident on the side of the road. Hearing the shot, he rushed to the scene, but there was nothing he could do. Once again, witnesses reported seeing a white van with two men inside leaving the area and heading for I-95.

Acting on a response plan they had worked out prior to the shooting, Virginia authorities shut down both Route 1 and I-95. Since I-95 is the major north–south highway on the East Coast, the resulting traffic jam was instant and massive.

Ordinarily, any police activity that resulted in the closing of I-95 anywhere between New York City and Richmond would cause a public uproar, and the telephones of politicians would be screaming with complaints. In this case, there were very few objections from the public. People were scared, and they looked to the police to catch the killers and put a stop to this nightmare. Yet it was a fruitless effort—the roadblocks and searches didn't provide any additional leads or information. Once again, the police were focused on a white van.

Within minutes of the latest shooting, the media swarmed to the scene. Media outlets from around the world were tuned to police radio communications, meaning that any police response or effort was immediately reported. Traffic reports were broadcasting locations of roadblocks. It doesn't take a genius to figure out that the killers were likely listening, and so knew which routes to avoid.

Back at the operations center, a hundred or so of us watched the news reports and live coverage from the scene. There didn't seem to be anything that any of us could do to help, a truly frustrating feeling. We were generating leads with the information we had, but were we wasting our time? There was no way of knowing the answer to that until the snipers were caught, which we all knew would happen sooner or later. My only question was, how many more people would have to die before we ran these monsters to ground?

One thing that struck me about this most recent shooting was that a state trooper was standing outside his patrol car less than fifty yards from the scene of Bridges's death. The shooters had to have seen the trooper. He would have been an easy target and an obvious opportunity for them, so why didn't they shoot him? Was the shooting of a citizen right under the noses of the police a message? Were they saying, "Look at us, we can kill who we want, when we want, even with the police standing nearby, and there's nothing you can do to stop us"? Or were they afraid to take on a police officer, who could shoot back? I think it was a combination. They liked to play God, and they chose a cowardly method—content to hide and shoot unarmed people who were powerless to fight back. Either way, it was a brazen act to shoot someone with a trooper so close by.

This thought actually gave me hope. The snipers were starting to get comfortable with what they were doing. It's one hell of a thing when the loss of a person's life gave me hope of finding these bastards, but comfort means mistakes. And mistakes meant that, sooner or later, we would get a break in the case. When a mistake did come, we needed to be on guard and looking for it.

When the preplanned roadblocks failed to turn up anything, I felt more strongly than ever that we were looking for the wrong vehicle. The roadblock searches had gone on for hours, and thousands of vehicles had been vetted, but once again the snipers simply merged back into the masses. They were hiding in plain sight, and we needed to get that tag check information from the various states and get it downloaded into Case Explorer, and it couldn't happen fast enough. The requests had been made, and the states and D.C. system administrators were working as quickly as possible to cull the requested information from their systems. Our HIDTA programmers were going at it nonstop, determined to make this work.

But our people were wearing out. We had been working around the clock for more than nine days. Besides getting little sleep, the troopers and civilian personnel under my command weren't eating well. They were stopping long enough to grab something off the catering table in the hallway and fill their coffee cups yet again. There was just so much work to do—the number of tips that had come in over the numerous tip lines was now well into five figures.

We had generated more than one hundred of what we considered "hot leads," each of which required our analysts to do complete background checks on the subject of the lead—and doing it in a few hours, not the usual two weeks of database searches and analysis such checks normally required.

The idle chat during breaks had stopped. There were no longer conversations concerning our kids, our families, our favorite restaurants. The pressure was mounting in all of us, right up to Captain McAndrew and me. It was the kind of pressure that can result in mistakes, and we couldn't afford that. We could not have our people so exhausted that they made poor decisions, or failed to notice something that was out of place.

It was time to order people to go home, take a day off, think about something other than this damn case. We all wanted to keep going until the killers were off the street, but this was no longer a sprint, it was a marathon. We had to be smart about how we used our team. We had to keep everybody fresh. Now more than ever, we needed them to be at their best.

So over the weekend of October 12–13, we ordered our troopers, civilian analysts, and programmers to take a day off. No more working longer than eight to ten hours a day, either. With no new weekend shootings—so far—we were able to take a few deep breaths and review what we had already done in such a short period of time. The goal was to tighten our processes and tie up loose ends left from the frenetic first few days.

I didn't take any days off, but I did limit myself to eight-hour shifts. I was able to go home, get some rest, spend some time with my family, and get a few good home-cooked meals. I hate to admit it, but I hadn't realized how important all of that was until this case came along. When I was in narcotics, I worked crazy hours and long shifts that sometimes had me in the field for three days at a stretch. I didn't think anything about it then, but I was younger, and there wasn't the same amount of pressure. Not like this.

But by Sunday evening, day eleven of the case, I was feeling rejuvenated, and my resolve was back full force. Though we had nothing new to hang our hats on, everybody's outlook had improved. What we didn't know, however, was that over the weekend Chief Ramsey of the Metro police had said in a scheduled press conference that his department was still interested in finding the older model burgundy Caprice that had been reported in a shooting in the city. Once again, that information never got passed to the Intelligence Division. No one working in or around the joint operations center knew about it. I'm not saying there was intentional withholding of information by any of the police agencies involved; the problem was just the sheer magnitude of the investigation. This case was like a centipede. It had a hundred legs, but too many of them were marching in different directions.

So, now, was the media. When there is nothing new to report, the press becomes more aggressive. Reporters were now beginning to follow investigators. At least that confusion was funny. We amused ourselves by gathering in a group at the lobby door just before leaving. This would get the press's attention. Then we would all run out, jump in our cars, and speed out of the parking lot in different directions. It never failed; heading out of the lot, I would look in the rearview mirror and see several press people running to their cars. It was fun watching them try to figure out which one of us to follow. On this particular Sunday evening, a reporter tailed me some thirty miles from Montgomery County well into Frederick County before finally figuring out that I wasn't running a hot lead; I was simply heading home.

20

October 14, 8:00 a.m., Monday. During a daily White House press briefing, President Bush's press secretary was asked about the sniper investigation. He said that the president was receiving daily briefings on the investigation, and that the White House was in constant contact with both federal and local law enforcement agencies. The press secretary emphasized that the president was very concerned.

We of course appreciated the president's interest in the case. The White House had been very supportive of our efforts and had seen to it that the full measure of federal resources was available to us. But of course presidential concern comes with a full measure of pressure as well. I had experienced pressure from elected officials to solve a case before, on other investigations. But there's nothing like pressure emanating from the White House. That produces a whole new level of stress.

So it was doubly dismaying that, at very nearly the same moment the press secretary was speaking, tragedy struck again. This time it was one of our own who fell victim to the sniper's bullet. FBI analyst Linda Franklin was with her husband at a Falls Church, Virginia, Home Depot and was loading her purchases into the back of her car. She was struck with a bullet from the same .223-caliber rifle, killing her instantly.

We had feared that a trooper or fellow officer would be targeted, but Franklin hadn't been involved in the sniper investigation, and none of the analysts working with us knew her. When she was shot, she wasn't wearing anything that would have identified her as FBI. Though we would go on to investigate any possible connection or motive that would have explained Franklin's being specifically targeted, the shooting appeared to be just as random as all the others. The snipers seemed to have killed a member of the law enforcement family without realizing it.

The location for this shooting was the most populated and crowded area yet. It was a bright, early fall morning, and there were other customers and employees walking in and out of the store, and plenty of parked vehicles in the parking lot. As police responded to the scene, roadblocks were quickly established. A witness told the police that he had seen the shooters. He described them as two white males driving a white van. His story was believable—his description of the vehicle matched previous descriptions, and the way he described the two white males fit the profile that had been broadcast and rebroadcast a hundred times over the past twelve days. Once again, the entire investigative team refocused on this mysterious white van. Several teams of investigators spent the next four days following up on the eyewitness account.

Yet only after the entire investigation was totally sidetracked did the truth come out. Under intense scrutiny, the witness admitted that he didn't see a thing. He admitted to doing it for the attention; he had just wanted to help. His help ended in his arrest for making a false statement and a false report to a police officer.

This really was nothing new and shouldn't have been a surprise to any of us. False reports and false leads from attention seekers happen quite often in high-profile cases. But the worst thing about attention-seeker statements is that their false leads eat up valuable police time and resources, giving the killers just that much more time to plot their next move.

Once we discounted the false witness, we were back where we had been before the Franklin killing. Other than the matching bullet, there simply was nothing in the form of evidence that could point this investigation in the right direction. Video cameras in and around the store and parking lot once again provided nothing of value. How could these killers stay so invisible?

The next four days were quiet, no additional shootings. Unfortunately, during that time we were unable to make any relevant progress. Following various leads, we had uncovered a multitude of other criminal offenses, but none had provided anything useful to the case we were trying to solve. While no one ever said it out loud, I know there was an underlying fear growing within the JOC: *Maybe we'll never find the killers.* What if they just stopped their killing and melted back into the population as easily as they had emerged? It wouldn't be the first time a psychopath serial killer had simply vanished, only to pop up years later in another city on the opposite side of the country.

One morning during the four-day reprieve, I took a break from the center along with Detective Sergeant Cornwell and a couple of civilian analysts. Our goal was to find some decent breakfast—we had just about had it with the cold cereal and Pop Tarts on the hallway catering tables. All of us had worked late the night before, and I had come back in early. It was obvious to me that the group needed to get out of the operations center and step away from the case for a while.

We got into my unmarked car and drove onto Rockville Pike, the main north-south drag in Montgomery County. On a normal weekday morning around 9 a.m., we should have had a hard time navigating through heavy morning traffic. Rockville Pike is lined with shopping centers, businesses, corporations, convenience stores, gas stations, and restaurants and is typically very, very busy. But now, as we headed to a nearby Denny's, the street was eerily quiet. Few people were out, other than patrol cars and the occasional delivery truck. It reminded me of the streets of an abandoned city in a zombie movie.

I pulled into the parking lot. A car and a truck were parked around the side, with no other cars in the lot. The restaurant blinds were drawn, and the place looked closed. Usually there were people sitting outside on the park benches waiting for a table, but not today. As I pulled into a parking space, I saw the Venetian blinds move in one of the windows. A young woman peeked out between the blinds. "What the hell?" I said, looking at Cornwell. "Has the entire region been paralyzed to the point that a chain restaurant is afraid to open?"

Cornwell looked out the window warily. "I don't know," he said. "But I've never seen anything like this before." He paused. "If we step out of this car, we're likely targets."

I exhaled hard. "Screw this," I said. "You can't live in fear, and you can't live forever," and I stepped out from behind the wheel of the car. I must admit that I was instantly scanning for anything that wasn't right—a glint of sun off a rifle scope, a door or trunk lid that wasn't completely closed. Anything. The hair was raised on the back of my neck.

The blinds closed, and I imagine the young woman must have been relieved when she saw us get out. I was in civilian business attire, my tie slightly loose around my neck, the top button of my shirt unbuttoned—but I was wearing a black raid-style jacket with the word POLICE boldly printed in a silver fluorescent material across my chest and back, and the state police patch was sewn on the top of each sleeve at the shoulder. The jacket covered my holstered .40-caliber Beretta sidearm. Cornwell was dressed similarly, except his tie was properly tight to his collar, and his top button was buttoned. Dan was always much more squared away than I was. He had come into the state police the same way we all had, but he was a technology guy and had begun his police career as a flight paramedic on one of our helicopters. He didn't have a lot of street or investigative experience, and he always made sure he looked good. As for me, fourteen years of working undercover in blue jeans, T-shirts, and baseball caps had clearly and permanently taken the shine off. I kept telling Dan that if he continued hanging out with me, I was sure that that state police polish of his would scuff up a bit.

The four of us walked into the restaurant. We were the only customers. Besides us, there were two waitresses and one cook in the entire place. The waitress who greeted us was about twenty-five years old. The look of relief on her face was evident.

"Not too busy today?" I asked.

"Just a few customers," she said. "I was afraid to come in to work, but I had to."

"Boss make you?"

"Single mom. I need the money."

She said that she and the other workers had closed all the blinds so the snipers couldn't see who was in the restaurant, or where they were. This was the first time that it had hit home to me *personally* how much of an effect the snipers were having on our entire community. Sure, I had seen the TV news reports about people crawling on their bellies while they put gas in their cars, but this was the first time I had stood face to face with a resident who was in fear.

While it was nice to get away from the operations center and enjoy some fresh, hot food, the four of us ate in silence. We weren't in the mood for small talk, and the outing did nothing to help us put the investigation out of our minds. In fact it was just the opposite. By the time we had finished eating, my temper was near the boiling point. *How dare these bastards hide in the bushes behind rifle sights? How dare they do this to our community—and, for that matter, to our country?* Our system felt truly fragile. The police are the thin blue line, but that line felt kind of threadbare at the moment.

On the way back to the operations center, I gave my friend Lieutenant Tom Chase of the Frederick City Police Department a call. I brought him up to speed on everything I knew, which wasn't much.

"Nothing new here, either," Chase said.

"Still," I said, "I can't help thinking these fuckers are laying their heads north of where the shootings are going down."

"So that would land them somewhere in Frederick County?"

"That's what I think. They started their killing in Montgomery County, then moved south into the District of Columbia before moving even farther south into Virginia. Then they moved back up I-95 and east into Prince George's County, where they shot the kid. It only makes sense that they would lie low in the direction where they haven't caused any trouble. Beyond what the FBI profilers have put out, that's where I'm at."

"I have to agree," Chase said. "Any word on the vehicle?"

"Nothing. Just that damn white van or truck we've been chasing with no luck. Honestly? I think we have the wrong vehicle. They may be gutless rat bastards, but they would have to be complete idiots to still be in that fucking white van—if they were ever in one in the first place. We would've turned something up by now. But this trail is too cold. These fuckers are street smart, Tom, and they have the cops chasing their own tails. And they're getting off on this shit."

"Yet everyone's reporting it," Chase said.

"Exactly. Even the public is on high alert. So why would they stay in a vehicle that's the most sought-after van in the country? It would take extreme stupidity . . . or extreme arrogance."

I told him about the emerging god complex that was manifesting as this thing progressed. "But the god complex that the killers obviously have might make them appear a little crazy, but not totally stupid," I added. "If they were stupid, what are we?"

I filled Chase in on our lead-production process, which had smoothed out considerably during the lull from the killings. We were still several days behind because of the sheer number of tips, but Case Explorer was working well, and we were successfully able to do the link analysis, matching names and information from the tips calls with criminal records, gun ownership, vehicle registration information, and other factors that fit our parameters.

I hung up as we pulled into the operations center parking lot. I couldn't help feeling a little depressed about what I had just told Chase. After all this time, and all we had done, there was still nothing positive that we could take out of it. The one bright spot was that the requested information concerning the police checks on vehicle tags was beginning to come in. The tech guys were working hard on converting the data into a usable format for Case Explorer, and Case Explorer was being adapted to analyze the data on the search pattern of one, three, and five miles out from each shooting, occurring from an hour before to an hour after each shooting.

That was a real challenge for the programmers, and they were getting close. I'm not a computer guy, and I don't know anything about the technical details of what they were doing, but even I knew that this should usually take months, if not years, to develop. These guys were doing it in less than a week. I worried about how long our programmers could hold up under this kind of pressure, with all the hours they were putting in and all the caffeine, candy bars, and sodas they were consuming. But they showed no signs of giving up, or quitting. At the moment, they were our best shot at getting to the bottom of this.

21

October 19, a Saturday, the seventeenth day of the nightmare. We were into our fifth day without a shooting, but the fear was still through the roof. Citizens were clearly altering their lives and staying out of view unless absolutely necessary. At the joint operations center, the lack of a shooting had a perverse, inverse effect: what if the killers had decided to stop their rampage? After our last witness had been discredited and locked up for filing a false report, the collective mood and morale of the task force were noticeably slipping.

Even the catered food reflected the dismal atmosphere—hot food like lasagna, spaghetti, and fried chicken had been replaced by skimpy sandwiches, small bags of chips, and off-brand cans of soda. The provisions were also indicative of our financial situation, of course; with each passing day, the resources needed to keep this massive investigative team together became that much further stretched.

But just as another frustrating, unproductive day turned into evening, Jeffrey Hopper was shot in the stomach as he and his wife came out of a Ponderosa Steakhouse restaurant just off I-95 in Ashland, Virginia. The shooting occurred at 7:19 p.m.—a little past dusk.

The steak house property consisted of a one-story building with a large parking lot wrapping the entire structure. There was outside lighting, though it was dim at best. But the Ponderosa Steakhouse had a feature that made the snipers' act easy. Behind the restaurant's parking area was a large wooded lot where the shot had come from. While Hopper would survive his injuries, neither he nor his wife saw anybody at the time of the shooting, and there was nothing suspicious to alert them.

Once again the Virginia State Police and the local sheriff's department quickly secured the area, setting up roadblocks and checkpoints all along not just I-95, but also Route 1, which is a heavily traveled option to the frequently congested interstate. As usual, traffic flow soon came to a virtual stop and resulted in massive traffic jams in all directions.

At the operations center, we continued working the leads that were being spit out of Case Explorer while also remaining glued to the live TV coverage. Just as they had with roadblocks after the previous shooting, the news crews were showing helicopter views of the massive traffic jams and were telling the public—along with the snipers—how to avoid the roadblocks and checkpoints. We watched, shaking our heads at the foolish media. More than one investigator shouted a few choice words at the TV. Yet there was nothing that could be done about the news coverage. The task force investigators were going to have to rely on the leadership to manage the press.

I called Captain McAndrew and briefed him on what we knew, which was exactly what anyone sitting in front of a TV set knew. McAndrew said he would see if he could get the latest information directly from Captain Forsyth; maybe there was something we could get a jump on that might start us down a new path.

And in fact this shooting would turn out to be different from the previous ones. After seventeen days, we were about to get the break we had been waiting for.

The crime scene investigative team swarmed the area surrounding the Ponderosa Steak House and quickly determined that the shot had come from a hiding place in the tree line at the rear of the restaurant. The location was a perfect sniper position. It was nestled in the woods well back from the parking lot, protecting the shooter from sight; but it also offered a clear view of the parking lot. The sniper had an unobstructed shooting lane directly to the spot where Hopper stood when he was hit.

Within minutes, investigators found a spent shell casing from the .223-caliber sniper rifle, which ultimately proved to be a Bushmaster assault-style rifle with a folding bipod barrel rest and optic sight system. And in a clear, zipped plastic bag tacked to the tree where the shooter had rested the rifle to take aim, the snipers had left the police a letter. Following evidence protocol, investigators carefully removed the bag from the tree, leaving the letter inside. The letter was then taken to the FBI forensics lab, where it was carefully removed from the plastic bag and examined for fingerprints before being read. This delayed our ability to read the letter right away, but it was the proper way to handle the evidence. Since we had nothing to indicate who the snipers were, we needed to go by the book—no quick examination of the letter would be done until we could do so under proper lab conditions, and when fingerprint evidence could be collected without fear of contamination. If this was the break in the case we had needed, we damn sure weren't going to get careless and screw it up.

This letter to the police was much more detailed than their previous communication, and that was the mistake that would finally allow us to put names to these killers. We also learned something from the form of the letter—the message was hand printed on lined, wide-rule notepaper, and affixed to the cover page were red star-shaped stickers like those a kindergarten teacher would dispense as a reward.

Once again it was clear that the snipers wanted the police to know they believed they had power over life and death. The god complex ran so deeply that they repeated the words "Call me God" in quotation marks on the first page of the letter. They also reiterated their warning not to release this letter to the press. The rest of the first page was devoted to calling out what they said was the incompetence of the police and the task force.

One disturbing revelation was that they had repeatedly phoned the task force and had finally spoken to someone on their fourth try. We knew we had a problem because of the heavy volume of calls coming in—there simply weren't enough lines to handle the traffic, and callers would get a busy signal. This problem had been acknowledged several times at public news conferences, and the public had been encouraged to keep on trying until the call went through and was answered. As the investigation progressed, additional phone numbers and hot lines were added almost daily to keep up with the call volume. This in turn hampered our ability to enter the info into Rapid Start and then into Case Explorer for analysis. As we had feared, some calls were going unlogged or were being lost in the system's inability to keep up.

Also, our trained call takers knew very little about the investigation beyond what everybody had gleaned from the media, so they were at a disadvantage in knowing when to be alert to something of interest a caller was telling them over the phone. It was just impossible to provide all those concerned with all the details they truly needed.

Besides calling the tip line, the snipers reported having called a priest in Ashland, Virginia, but the priest didn't take their call seriously. They had also called D.C. Metropolitan Police. On the first page of their letter they said that law enforcement's "failure to respond has cost you five lives." Once again, they were blaming us for their killings. To the cops reading this, it was like having salt rubbed into an open wound. Their words sent me into hyper drive. I damn sure wasn't going to quit until the case either was solved or killed me. As I looked into the faces of the team around me, I knew I wasn't alone.

On page two, they switched from telling us how incompetent we were to demanding money. They wanted $10 million. In order to stop the killing, we were to deposit that amount into a Bank of America platinum Visa account in the name of Jill Lynn Farell, for which the killers provided the account number and PIN. The account was to be activated so that they could access it from anywhere in the world. The terms, they said, were not negotiable. We were given until 9 a.m. Monday to complete the transaction.

On page three, the snipers said they would call us Sunday morning at six to confirm that their terms were acceptable. Once again, they placed the blame for any future killings on the police.

They closed their letter with a postscript: *P.S. Your children are not safe anywhere at any time.*

22

This letter provided us a wealth of information that could be quickly verified and followed up on. And ironically, for what seemed like the first time during the investigation, the press didn't learn of the letter's existence. In fact, few people within the task force knew about this letter, and even fewer knew what was in it.

Almost from the start, we had believed that these crimes weren't committed by a single shooter. Now we had confirmation—they had referred to themselves as "us." We also now could rest assured that this wasn't an organized plot. The letter had included the childish red stars; no terrorist would pen a letter to the police and adorn it with stickers that undermined the seriousness of their message. Another clue to their lack of sophistication—the killers wanted $10 million deposited into a Visa credit card account. Even if we wanted to give these morons $10 million, there was no way it could be done on a credit card. The account holder's name and account number in the letter also represented a very significant lead. A credit card meant there was an electronic trail associated with it. We figured that the card owner, Jill Lynn Farell, was a likely crime victim—possibly of a previous homicide not yet connected to the killers, or the victim of a theft or robbery. Either way, the card number could easily be traced to where it originated and where it had been used since it was stolen.

The calls referenced in the letter also proved to be of significant help. Just as we had feared, the killers' calls to our task force hadn't been properly entered into Rapid Start, but we had a good lead on their call to a priest in Ashland. Moving quickly, investigators were able to identify the priest and interview him. He said he had received a call from a man identifying himself as the sniper. The caller told the priest that the police should be looking in "Montgomery" at a "liquor store robbery." The priest admitted that he hadn't taken the call seriously and hadn't reported it to authorities; he thought his caller was just another troubled soul wanting to confess his sins or get credit for being the Beltway sniper.

We didn't blame him. As I said before, there are a lot of troubled souls out there looking for attention. Responding to these calls is like dealing with the man in the theater who habitually yells "fire." After being fooled the first few times, people stop listening. Then when there really is a fire, nobody pays attention, and everybody burns to death. The priest should have called the police after his phone conversation with the man who turned out to be one of the snipers, but would we have picked up right away on this tip? Or would we have lumped it in with the thousands of other calls we would eventually need to get to?

After interviewing the priest, investigators turned their attention to Montgomery County. What would have been so significant about a liquor store robbery? There had been several liquor store robberies in the county, but, on the surface, none appeared to have any characteristics that would have matched with the sniper case.

I don't know who realized it, but it soon dawned on investigators that they might be looking in the wrong "Montgomery"— maybe the snipers weren't referring to Montgomery County, Maryland. So investigators began searching the national crime databases, homing in on other Montgomerys. Eventually they ran across a case that loosely fit the profile and style of the Beltway snipers: on September 21, 2002—less than two weeks before the first shooting through the window of that Michaels store in Maryland—a woman was shot in the face, execution style, as she exited a liquor store in Montgomery, Alabama.

Digging deeper, investigators learned that the victim, an employee of the liquor store, was walking out of the store when she was approached by two unidentified black males. Without saying a word, one of the men pulled a pistol and shot her in the face. The bullet passed through the victim's head and shattered the large front window of the liquor store. Clerks working inside reported seeing the men running from the scene. As they fled, they dropped the pistol, and other witnesses saw a folded magazine falling out of the pocket of one of the men.

Law enforcement in Montgomery, Alabama, never entered this case into the FBI's VICAP database. A VICAP entry is voluntary on the part of investigating police agencies, and there can be any number of reasons for a particular case not being entered. Budgetary constraints always loom large, and voluntary programs such as VICAP are often sacrificed in favor of applying human resources to the demands of basic needs. But of course this was another missed opportunity. Early in the investigation, we had linked VICAP to Case Explorer. With our sketchy evidence on the sniper investigation, Case Explorer might never have made the link to that brutal murder in Alabama; we will never know. But if it *had* made that link, we would have saved at least twenty-four hours, and that could well have saved someone's life. This is the kind of thing that eats at the soul of every investigator.

As crime scene techs worked the Alabama shooting site that night in September, they collected the gun and the magazine. There was nothing useful found on the gun—no prints or identifiers. But investigators were able to lift a single fingerprint from a page in a *Guns & Ammo* magazine the snipers had been looking through. This was a rare find. Despite popular belief, perpetuated by decades of crime and police dramas, criminals are rarely identified and crimes solved on the basis of one fingerprint. In fact, lifting good, usable prints at all is a huge challenge. Most of the time there are no usable prints because the criminals wear gloves. Or they slide their hands across objects, smearing the prints. Or the things they touch aren't suitable for obtaining a clean print. But it just so happens that the glossy paper used to publish magazines is *perfect* for collecting fingerprint evidence.

So the evidence techs got lucky. But the next hurdle in using a fingerprint to identify a suspect is that the recovered print needs to match a set of prints that have already been entered in one of the many fingerprint files maintained at both the federal and state level. Anytime a person is arrested, a full set of fingerprints is saved on an FBI fingerprint card and submitted to the FBI lab in West Virginia. Criminal record checks through NCIC are based on forwarding fingerprint cards and arrest information to the FBI. If the suspect was never arrested or fingerprinted, your record check will hit a dead end.

In addition to the FBI system, every state has its own fingerprint database. Depending on the individual state laws and procedures, prints are kept for such transactions as gun purchases, handgun permits, and security clearances, as well as for job applications for teachers, day-care center operators, and child-care workers. Because these records aren't related to a criminal offense, they are not kept in the FBI file. There are also other fingerprint databases, such as the one the U.S. Citizenship and Immigration Services maintains on illegal aliens or other noncitizens who have come in contact with Immigration.

At the time of their investigation into the liquor store murder, law enforcement in Montgomery, Alabama, ran the single lifted fingerprint from the *Guns & Ammo* magazine against the FBI database but did not receive a match. They didn't go on to conduct a nationwide search, however, so their print remained on file only locally.

Now, because of the possibility that the Alabama case was related to the Beltway sniper case, we ran that lone print against all the fingerprint databases nationwide. It would take time for the computer system to return anything, of course, and then those records would have to be checked and verified by fingerprint comparison experts. But within a few hours we had a match. The task force had our first name. Eventually, we would have a face to go with it.

23

Lee Boyd Malvo was identified as a juvenile illegal alien, born February 18, 1985, in Kingston, Jamaica. His print had been identified through the Citizenship and Immigration fingerprint database. Malvo had been deported to his native Jamaica seven years prior. He was now seventeen years old.

Additional information and pictures of the suspect were immediately requested from immigration officials, and an FBI investigative team was dispatched to Montgomery, Alabama, to collect any additional information and to start following leads from there. *Now* we had something to help us link the leads provided by the killers in their letter. We started with the credit card they wanted to use to get their $10 million. Credit cards are easily traced because of the electronic footprint they leave everywhere they are used. The owner of the card turned out to be a long-distance bus driver. When questioned, she said the card had been stolen from her the previous March while she was driving the bus through Arizona.

Now we had the beginnings of a trail. We knew the killers had been in Arizona and Montgomery, Alabama. The investigative team went into a full-court press, tracking Lee Boyd Malvo to find out who he was, where he had been, and whom he was traveling with. Over the next several days, the FBI and investigators from the SNIPMUR task force would pursue multiple leads and conduct extensive interviews all over the country.

We would discover that Lee Boyd Malvo was traveling with a person who was believed to be some sort of mentor to him. John Allen Muhammad had befriended young Malvo and had, according to some accounts, taken Malvo under his wing—sometimes even referring to Malvo as his son. Muhammad, who was born John Allen Williams in Baton Rouge, Louisiana, on December 31, 1960, was a former soldier who had made it to the rank of sergeant. His military career was average at best, and he possessed no particular skills that would raise any eyebrows or alarms.

Muhammad was tracked to the state of Washington, near Tacoma. He had been married to a Mildred Muhammad, who had divorced him and taken the kids into hiding. Ironically, she had moved with the children to Maryland—a fact that Muhammad was unaware of. Mildred may have been in hiding for good reason. In February 2002, Keenya Cook was shot and killed when she answered the front door to her Tacoma home. That homicide remained unsolved—there was no clear motive for the crime. But as the pieces of this case began to fit together, we discovered that Keenya Cook was a friend of Muhammad's ex-wife Mildred. She was believed to be the person who had helped Mildred take the kids and disappear to Maryland.

That was just the start of what we were uncovering about Muhammad and Malvo. They were tracked to a former residence, also near Tacoma, where the two had lived together. Neighbors told investigators that Muhammad and Malvo had spent time firing some sort of rifle into a stump in the backyard. Further investigation found that, during their travels, Muhammad and Malvo had purchased a Bushmaster .223-caliber rifle from a gun shop in California. Investigators, armed with search-and-seizure warrants, went to their former house near Tacoma and removed the stump from the property for examination. Bullets were dug out of the stump.

Another thing investigators uncovered: In late 2001, John

Muhammad had bought an old Caprice, with well over one hundred thousand miles on it, from an auto sales dealer in Trenton, New Jersey. He registered the car in his name and, according to New Jersey DMV records, was displaying current New Jersey tags—NDA-21Z. Now that we knew what trail to follow, the task force was all over it.

October 20, 2002, Sunday. For the first time in eighteen days, this didn't feel like just another day of beating our heads against the wall. The investigation had gone from frustration to a frenzy of activity, and I finally felt we were on the right track. I now had confidence that we would soon bring this case to a close and put a stop to the shootings and killings. Since we were now aware of the snipers' attempt to contact the task force, all call centers had been put on full alert, with instructions to immediately put through to the JOC any call from a caller identifying himself as the sniper. That meant we would chase any such call, even if it later turned out to be a dead end.

As the snipers had indicated in their letter, early that Sunday morning the joint operations center had received a call traced to a public telephone at a gas station not far from the Ponderosa Steak House. The callers, who identified themselves as the snipers, were checking in—they wanted to make sure the police had found their note.

This was it. Since the existence of the letter had successfully been kept from the press, we knew it had to be the snipers. Police units quickly converged on the area where the call had originated; ironically, they found a white van with three people in it sitting near the public phone. A few short minutes of excitement and anxiety later, we determined that these weren't our snipers. The three guys in the van had nothing to do with the case; they had simply stopped at the gas station near the bank of public phones. Unfortunately, they hadn't seen anyone using the phones.

On Sunday afternoon, Chief Moose, in an effort to get the snipers to make direct contact with the task force—and hopefully to set another trap—met with the media camped in front of police headquarters. Speaking directly to the snipers through the media, Chief Moose said, "The person you called could not hear everything that you said. The audio was unclear, and we want to get it right. Call us back so that we can clearly understand."

Then, trying to prevent another shooting and to gain trust with the snipers, he repeated their words from the letter: "Word is bond." The media, suspecting something significant had happened or was about to happen, peppered the chief with questions concerning what he had just said on camera. The chief didn't bite. Instead, he said, several times, that it would be "inappropriate" to comment on the ongoing investigation, and ended the press conference.

We watched the coverage with considerable amusement, as the media launched into an orgy of speculation. TV anchors accused the police of "using" the media, and the views expressed ranged from outrage to justification that the media should be used to help capture the criminals. "Finally," I said to Cornwell, "those TV bastards are getting a taste of their own medicine. Now maybe they might actually be useful."

"Yeah," said Cornwell, "like lipstick on a pig." We both laughed. It was the first time in quite a while that we had been able to let loose and really laugh.

No matter what opinion the media took of their usefulness or their being used, they all paraded the usual host of experts in front of the cameras—retired military generals, retired FBI agents, retired homicide detectives from New York and LA, and, of course, psychologists. Every one of them was trying to "explain" what the task force was doing. Despite being entertaining to those of us on the inside of the investigation, all this press coverage did nothing to lessen the pressure we were under.

While we felt closer than ever to the finish line, we also knew we were still too damned far from it. Few of us wanted to leave the center to get a sandwich, let alone to go home for a shower, a change of clothes, or a night's rest. We had come this far and wanted to be present when the end came. After eighteen days, we were like bloodhounds that had finally found the scent.

It was a giant leap to finally have a couple of names and, very soon, faces, but that was only a first step. It was still a massive operation to find those two faces among the millions of people living, working, and traveling through two states and the city of Washington. We worked through the night, poring again over reams of information that we had already reviewed, looking for any reference to the two names we had, or to the Caprice.

Now we could use that license plate number to try to connect Muhammad and Malvo to each shooting. As I had said in the meeting, every good cop runs license plate checks on cars that catch his eye for one reason or another, and now data on those plate checks from the various systems had been converted to a format that Case Explorer could work with. Over Sunday and into Monday, we ran the search for common tag numbers that police had seen and checked on around each shooting.

———

Monday, October 21, 5:56 a.m. While we dug through information and ran our Case Explorer search, other investigative teams, including uniformed officers and troopers on the road, fanned out across the region in anticipation of the killers' calling again. If they did, we hoped the call could be traced a little quicker, giving our teams in the field a better chance to collar the snipers.

In the meantime, Conrad Johnson was preparing his Ride-On Bus for his daily run. He was sitting in the parked bus along a pull-off in Silver Spring, Maryland, in Montgomery County, the second bus in a line of several buses. It was 5:56 a.m., and in a few minutes, he would begin his morning route. Then a shot rang out from a wooded area next to where his bus was parked. A bullet flew through the open bus door and struck Johnson, killing him instantly.

Police units responded quickly, and a perimeter was established around the scene within minutes. Other bus drivers and witnesses reported seeing a masked man running through the woods in the direction the shot had come from and into an apartment complex on the other side of the wooded lot. Police descended on the woods and the apartment complex, searching the hundreds of apartments in the multi-building complex. But once again the snipers had slipped away.

Not without leaving something behind, however: another letter was found in the woods. Just like the last letter, this one was in a plastic bag and was covered with little red star stickers. The letter was short, direct, and angry in tone: *For You Mr. Police Call me God do not release to the press.* It also contained the same ominous warning as the last letter: *your children are not safe.*

This letter clearly indicated that the killers were pissed at the police. They demanded respect: *Can you hear us now! Do not play these Childish games with us. You know our demands next person (your choice) Thank you.*

24

October 21, Monday, 8 a.m. The letter didn't come as a surprise to any of us working on the task force. The snipers were trying to show us that they were in charge. They were angry that their deadline had passed without their stolen credit card being activated so they could access their $10 million. They wanted us to know that the killing of Conrad Johnson was the result of our refusal to show them respect or to bow to their demands. Now they repeated those demands and said, essentially, that the next victim was up to us—and their postscript indicated that they would target another child. The stakes in this case were already the highest of any investigation I had ever been involved in. And after more than twenty years in law enforcement, I knew that the snipers' letter would have the opposite effect of what they intended. Troopers do not bow to threats.

In an effort to prevent what we all feared was about to happen, Chief Moose once again conducted a press conference in front of his headquarters in Rockville. Not surprisingly, the press was all over the killing of Conrad Johnson. News crews were closely monitoring the comings and goings of cops in and about the operations center, and they could tell something was happening. Cops were coming, but not leaving. There wasn't the usual smaller number of personnel at night.

Visibly exhausted and emotional, Chief Moose once again spoke directly to the snipers, using the mass media coverage as a communications tool. He played to their god complex, and he tried to de-escalate the anger that was expressed in their latest letter. He announced to the public that he could not assure the safety of anybody.

Watching his press conference, I felt sorry for Moose. How does any law enforcement officer stand in front of the media and tell the public—which he, like all of us, had taken a solemn oath to defend and protect—that they were not safe, that he could not assure their safety? It's our job to make the public *feel* safe. Of course we know we can't possibly protect every single person, but it's still a very bitter pill for a police chief to have to go on live television and admit it. Chief Moose did what he needed to do, though: he needed to placate the killers and hopefully stop them—or at least delay them—from killing again. He was buying us time.

And maybe it would be enough. By now Case Explorer had created another lead for us. During seven of the shootings, a blue Caprice with New Jersey tags NDA-21Z had been spotted within a five-mile radius of the crime scenes and within an hour before or after the shootings. My hunch that cops had seen these guys and run the tags had been correct. The snipers had drawn the suspicions of police. But since the tags had come back valid, with no wants or warrants, there was no reason to stop them. We were all looking for a white van or truck, not a blue Caprice. That's how the snipers had been able to drive through the roadblocks and lookouts unchallenged.

The reports of a Caprice, which had been mentioned at two of the shootings, had never made it to our radar. In hindsight, that looms as a huge mistake. The problem was partly that the investigation spanned two states and the District of Columbia, and information sharing back then was nothing like it is today. But we can't discount our own culpability. We had become blindly focused on a white van or truck, convinced that all those witnesses who had kept reporting such vehicles *had* to be right.

Now that we could put that Caprice at or around several of the shooting scenes, however, we began conducting further record checks to see if this tag had been run by any other police officer, anywhere, at any time. Sure enough, during the first week of the shooting spree a Baltimore City Police officer had spotted the car parked in an alley in Baltimore with two people in it. The officer had run the tag because where the car was parked and the two people in it seemed suspicious. But the vehicle had checked out as properly registered and not reported stolen, and a routine ID check showed that neither occupant was wanted for anything. So the officer shooed them out of the alley, and the killers went on their way. This also confirmed my suspicion that while they were doing their killing in Montgomery and Prince George's County in Maryland, in D.C., and in Northern Virginia, they were lying low in the opposite direction. Since they had been rousted once in Baltimore, I was convinced that they were now in my neighborhood—Frederick County.

By Tuesday morning, the bullets removed from the stump in Washington State had been matched ballistically to the rifle used in the killings in the D.C. Metro area. Plus, we were working at placing the blue Caprice at or near the scene of the shootings, and we were still waiting final confirmation on the fingerprint match from Alabama. The task force, as a whole, was working all across the country to firm up what we suspected. We wanted enough evidence and probable cause to seek these guys out and legally take them into custody.

But we had to be especially careful to make sure our evidence had been collected properly and examined thoroughly, and that an ironclad chain of custody for that evidence was maintained. Everything had to survive any legal challenge that some defense attorney down the road might mount. Evidence collected in the field and analyzed over weeks could come down to collection and storage methods. Since evidence was coming in from all over the country, primary investigators needed to mount a coordinated effort that was documented in a meticulously detailed and straightforward manner. That takes time. It's easy, as an investigator, to want to go, go, go, especially under the pressure of trying to prevent further killing. But speed could also hurt us. Everything *had* to be done correctly so that when we did get them, we could get them off the street forever, guilty beyond any reasonable doubt.

In the afternoon, Chief Moose again took center stage at another news conference, still trying to buy us the time we needed to firm up our case. He released the postscript of the first letter: "your children are not safe any time or anywhere." Public fear grew. Meanwhile, the press didn't understand what Moose was trying to do. A few wondered if the police were now being played like puppets by the killers. Little did they know that Chief Moose's words were the result of much discussion and many years of law-enforcement training. Experts deeply involved in the investigation, including profilers, were advising the chief on what he should and shouldn't say.

Meanwhile, inside the JOC, tensions were rising. That is natural as a case comes close to conclusion. Of course there's excitement, but sometimes emotions take a negative turn. That was clear during a meeting in a conference room at the JOC later that day. Most of us there had been in this room more than we had been home in the last three weeks. Like the hastily assembled operations center itself, the men and women in the room looked like a mixed bag of doughnuts. Some were in business attire; the FBI agents had their jackets on and their ties straight. Detectives from the Montgomery County Police Department were jacketless, as was I. Our ties were hanging loose, with the top buttons of our shirts unbuttoned. Several in the room wore black BDUs (battle dress uniforms) and were fully armed, with tactical holsters and boots.

Despite how we looked as a group, all of us had one thing in common: we were exhausted. We, along with some nine hundred other cops, had spent the better part of twenty-two days, most of us working sixteen- to eighteen-hour days, using our collective experience, energy, and tenacity in an effort to identify and bring to justice the Beltway snipers. This new task force had come together and was working as a cohesive unit.

Up until this moment.

The purpose of this meeting of the task force leadership was to make sure that our information was correct and to form a plan. After twenty-two days of intense investigation, we now knew who the killers were. We had names, and we had a vehicle license number. It was go time.

My eyes were glazing over. I was tired, but that wasn't it. I couldn't believe what I was hearing. Two federal agents, who oversaw their respective agencies (FBI and ATF), were arguing over who was going to release the information or BOLO. I looked at Captain Bernie Forysth, Montgomery County Police Department, the lead investigator for the case. I knew what he was thinking—how could we have come so far so well and now be arguing over who gets to appear before the sea of media waiting outside the joint operations center? We had known it was coming—how could it not? This was a high-profile case. Egos were taking over. Now, as we were closing in, the agencies were wrestling for control.

There is a long-standing joke among local and state law enforcement about the FBI: Three K-9 officers and their K-9 partners are standing in front of a residence preparing to serve a search-and-seizure warrant. One officer is a county officer and his dog, one officer is a state trooper and his dog, and the third is a federal agent and his dog.

The county guy says to the other two, "Watch this." He sends his dog into the house and you hear cussing and screaming and furniture crashing. After a few minutes, the dog comes out and throws a package containing a kilo of cocaine at his handler's feet. The deputy says, "What do you think about that?"

"That's very good," says the trooper, "but watch this." He sends his dog into the same house and you hear more cussing, screaming, and crashing furniture. After a few minutes, the dog comes out of the house and gently lays an explosive device at the feet of the trooper. The trooper says, "Now what do you think about that?"

The federal agent looks at the other two and says, "That's nothing, watch this." His dog walks over and screws the other two dogs, then puts out a press release.

I used to find that joke hilarious, but somehow it didn't seem so funny now.

———

Late in the afternoon Chief Moose addressed the snipers in a third press conference of that very busy day. "We have researched the options you stated," he said, "and found it is not possible electronically to comply in the manner that you requested. However, we remain open and ready to talk to you about the options you have mentioned. It is important that we do this without anyone else getting hurt. Call us at the same number you used before to obtain the eight hundred number that you have requested. If you would feel more comfortable, a private post office box or another secure method could be provided. You indicated that this is about more than violence. We are waiting to hear from you."

Chief Moose was doing his best to make the snipers believe they were in control—that they were eventually going to get their $10 million. The thinking was that if we could buy just a little more time, we could get these guys. But we also knew that if they went off the rails in anger, more people were going to die in the process.

As the twentieth day of the investigation slowly turned into the twenty-first day, none of us working the intelligence side of the case had gone home for three days. As viable information became available, we picked up our pace. None of us wanted this investigation to fail because the intelligence group had dropped the ball. There was no way in hell I would quit or stop longer than to go to the bathroom, and nobody on my team would quit either.

I remember looking at Detective Sergeant Cornwell. "Dan," I said, "you look like hell."

"You don't look any better than I do," he said. "I know you're not going home, so I'm not, either."

I had been sending people home over the past several days only to see them back a few hours later, bent over their computers reviewing leads and evaluating what Case Explorer was spitting out. These cops, troopers, agents, and civilian analysts who had come together for this case were giving it everything they had. They were unsung heroes—they and the other nine-hundred-plus people working on this case. Whether we met with success or failure, I was damn proud to be part of this group.

But there comes a point when working without rest brings diminishing results. We had reached that point, and productivity was slipping. On October 23 at 1 a.m., Detective Sergeant Cornwell, Captain McAndrew, and I ordered everybody on duty to go home for a few hours, get some sleep, and be back in the morning ready to go for what we all hoped was the final push. We now had an idea of who the killers were and what they might be driving. We needed to turn that idea into proof.

Then we had to go out there and find what rock these scumbags were hiding under before even more people were killed.

The losses so far were already unacceptable, and even though we had sent our people home, I didn't plan to go. But Captain McAndrew had other ideas. He knew me about as well as anybody else on the MSP. "You really need to go home," he said. "And if nothing else, do everybody a favor and take a shower."

25

At any given time, the Maryland State Police has approximately fourteen hundred sworn members on staff. All are capable of performing multiple police tasks, and in fact are expected to. Once they have received the basic training that every trooper gets, there are a number of specialties that they can enter into, including aviation and flight paramedic, homicide investigator, narcotics trooper, or—the unit I was heading up during the sniper nightmare—criminal intelligence. As young troopers' skills are developed, the Maryland State Police provides excellent opportunities for training and honing those skills, based upon what each trooper likes to do balanced against the needs of the agency.

But whatever our current assignment or job responsibilities may be, we are all expected to react and respond as we were trained to do. We are trained to remain calm and in control during any crisis that may crop up. When a crisis occurs, from multiple-car accidents to homicide or hostage barricade situations, that first trooper on the scene is expected to take command, evaluate the situation, and report back to the barrack and his or her command to relay what's going on, what's needed, and then take the appropriate action. "One riot, one trooper" is a phrase that was drilled into me from day one in the academy. Troopers ride alone, and in most of the rural areas a trooper's closest backup may be twenty minutes away, or even farther. So a trooper must make spur-of-the-moment, sometimes life-or-death decisions within the guidelines of police training and the laws of Maryland. A trooper who can't make those decisions won't make it as a road trooper in Maryland—or in any state police agency in the United States, for that matter.

Troopers have to trust in their training and experience. They have to have the self-assurance to stand fast in the face of any situation, and to get the job done. Likewise, supervisors and commanders have to trust those troopers under their command; they can't second guess or countermand something the trooper was doing unless they themselves are on the scene to make the call. It's also critical for supervisors and commanders to know the troopers they serve with. They have to know what skills each trooper has, and to avoid placing troopers in situations that they aren't capable of handling. If there's no other option, it's on the trooper to attend to his or her duty. For example, a trooper who is a criminal investigator might happen upon an accident scene, in which case the trooper is expected to stop, render aid, and secure the scene until a uniformed trooper arrives. The same can be said for the uniformed road trooper who comes across a homicide scene. He or she must render aid, protect the scene and evidence, and, if the suspect is present, make an arrest. The trooper must also maintain control and handle the investigation until properly relieved by a criminal investigator. For any trooper, this is all in a day's work. One of our mottos is, "Take no grief / Cut no slack / Hook 'em and book 'em / And don't look back."

When I was a young trooper patrolling the road out of the

Frederick Barrack, I reported to an experienced senior sergeant. Once, when I just wasn't sure of myself concerning an arrest I was working on, I went to him and asked what I needed to do. The sergeant looked me hard in the eye. "The citizens of Maryland gave you a badge, a gun, bullets, a cruiser, and the best police training that is available," he said. "Make a decision, son, show some balls, and get the damn job done."

That lesson had stuck with me throughout my career, and it would come into play as we drew nearer to catching the Beltway snipers.

One of the units the Maryland State Police deploys is the Special Tactical Assault Team Element, or STATE. When I first started out as a trooper in the early '80s, the STATE team was made up of specially trained and extremely fit troopers—primarily road troopers—from all over Maryland. Experts in special weapons and assault tactics, they are the state police version of a SWAT team, called upon to respond to hostage barricade situations, high-risk search-and-seizure warrants, and other such events or situations on an as-needed basis. Each six-person team gets backup from its own command staff, and they have special equipment that is strategically placed around the state for deployment. There is always one team on call, with another in standby mode, in case two teams are needed.

As need for the skills of the STATE teams expanded during the '80s, amid the violence associated with the so-called war on drugs, the teams morphed from part-time to full-time units, which helped further increase their capabilities. As each team is deployed, it comes with its own on-call command staff and specialized equipment. Upon a STATE team's arrival at any situation, the command and control of the incident is turned over to that team, and the local barrack personnel fall into a backup and perimeter guard role. Over the years, I had worked closely with just about every trooper who is a member of the STATE team, and I had come up through the ranks with all their command staff. These troopers and their leaders are the very best of the Maryland State Police. I've served many high-risk search-and-seizure warrants with them, and I would put them up against any other law enforcement team in the country, including the FBI.

During my years working narcotics, it was clear that what once would have been considered a low- or medium-risk serving of a search-and-seizure warrant could now escalate to high-risk in a split second. Many of us believe there's no such thing as a low-risk search-and-seizure warrant. Despite our best efforts in gathering all the intelligence and background concerning a search-and-seizure target, you never know what violence the bad guys are capable of until they're cornered. I've seen suspects who were known to be extremely violent throw their hands up and proclaim, "You got me." I've also seen suspects with no criminal record or known background for violence come out fighting—even be willing to die before submitting to arrest. Many times in the early '80s we would hit crack houses and stash houses with search-and-seizure warrants served by only me and one or two other narcs, along with some poor uniformed cop who happened to be on duty. Knowing what I know now, we were extremely lucky that none of us was ever killed or seriously injured serving warrants—understaffed and half-assed as we were, as we in the state police like to put it.

For sure I was lucky when, as a young trooper working the road in Frederick County, I was called in to assist the narcs with a search warrant. When I arrived at the barrack, I was told to do whatever they needed—I was to be the "uniform presence" for the warrant service. Soon I met Detective Sergeant Peter Edge, who was in charge of the Westminster Barracks Criminal Investigation

Section at the time. Edge gave me simple instructions: follow them to an address across the street from the barrack and go up on the front porch with the server and knock on the door and announce that it was the state police with a warrant. Edge said I was there only so the bad guys would see that it was the real police. Looking around the room, I realized what he meant. The office was full of guys with long hair and beards—hippie cops wearing jeans, T-shirts, and ball caps emblazoned with Orioles, Yankees, and Harley Davidson logos. Little did I know that I would eventually spend a decade and a half of my career looking just like them.

Instructions done, we went across the street, and I knocked on the door. Instantly, a massive shootout started, with bad guys firing at us from both inside and outside the house. Bullets were flying. At least one round hit the wooden door trim, just inches above my Stetson—a shot that was fired through a window from the inside. It was then that I realized I was the only readily identifiable target out there. In those days, we didn't have raid jackets and hats with POLICE emblazoned on them; instead, there was just that ragtag collection of baseball hats. I didn't know who to shoot at, so I jumped off the porch and got under it, followed quickly by Detective Sergeant Edge. He looked at me, saw the panic and confusion in my face, and said in a calm voice, "This is a fucking mess; this was supposed to be easy."

Years later we still hadn't learned those early lessons. We still were hitting houses and serving warrants with only a couple of us and a uniform. Every time, we thought it was going to be easy, but far too often we would burst into some building, house, or apartment only to be confronted by ten or more armed people— in over our heads just like that. Sometimes we had to fight our way in, and occasionally in the bad neighborhoods in Charm City (Baltimore) we had to fight our way back out with prisoners and a haul of cocaine or heroin. It was probably only due to dumb luck that we never lost a trooper doing this kind of thing.

Eventually we wised up. Because the Narcotics Division was serving so many search-and-seizure warrants at multiple locations nearly every day, we had to tighten up our act. As a result, the STATE teams began training the rest of us to serve search-and-seizure warrants. We certainly weren't trained to the level the STATE teams were, but we implemented their basic method— meaning, first of all, that we would never serve any search warrant with anything less than a six-person team. We were taught how to gain entry and, working with a partner, and in three teams of two, clear an entire house and take control of anybody who was found inside the target location. I saw firsthand how STATE worked as a team and what they needed any other troopers on the perimeter to do. I learned that no matter what we heard—gunshots, flash-bang grenades, or shouting and screaming, we were *not* to come in, but to maintain weapons discipline and to hold the perimeter while they did their job—which they did every time.

All these lessons that I had learned over the years, and all that I had practiced, taught, and preached as a commander, would now be vitally important to me. The last day of the Beltway sniper investigation was about to begin.

STATE teams were being utilized daily to assist in the securing of the schools in Montgomery County. Also, since multiple agencies were involved in the SNIPMUR task force, we had worked on cross training with SWAT teams from Montgomery County and the FBI. Once we cornered the suspects, it was likely going to end in a violent confrontation. One-on-one, the snipers had every uniformed police officer, trooper, or agent outgunned. And since the snipers had proven their ability to kill at will, there was good reason to think they wouldn't go down without a fight. With their obvious god complex, they felt invincible and thought they were much smarter than the police.

The Maryland State Police STATE team commander was the same Major Jim Ballard who had called me and alerted me on the first day of the investigation that something unusual was happening. He was now doubling as regional commander for the state police. This was a stroke of luck for us. Major Ballard was respected among both Montgomery County SWAT team members and the FBI special tactical teams.

During the first twenty days of this investigation, Ballard had coordinated the Maryland State Police uniform response as well as the protection efforts at the schools in Montgomery County. In his spare time, he helped with the combined training among state police, FBI, and Montgomery County SWAT teams, aiming to hone them into a single unit. The various team members got to know one another and learned to account for the differences in each agency's training. As a combined unit, they prepared and trained for the unknown. They tried to create every scenario they could think of, from a traffic stop or a hostage barricade situation to a manhunt for heavily armed suspects in the woods. Then they practiced how they would operate in each situation—a next-to-impossible task.

Major Ballard feared, as did the rest of us, that sooner or later a road trooper or county officer was going to stop the killers in a routine traffic stop or checkpoint and would be outgunned. In an attempt to counter the imbalance, the teams formed into three-person traffic backup teams, known as TANGO teams. Each TANGO team consisted of a STATE team member, an FBI SWAT team member, and a Montgomery County police SWAT team member. The TANGO teams deployed throughout the Montgomery County and metropolitan area. Their job was to monitor all traffic stops being made and immediately serve as backup officers to assist in the traffic stops. We were dealing with an unknown killer with unknown training, so the TANGO teams wore full tactical gear and were heavily armed. Their appearance was intimidating, and was meant to be. How this impending confrontation played out was going to be completely up to the killers.

26

October 23, 5:30 a.m. The day started like every day of the past three weeks had. For me, it began with about three hours of sleep, a shower, and Pop Tarts and a granola bar for breakfast. Nothing different—except for a renewed hope that we were finally on the killers' trail and it was only a matter of time until the assembled posse of nearly a thousand law enforcement officers found them and closed the noose around their necks. As I climbed into car 662 and headed south on I-270 back to the operations center, I was hoping to hear over the police radio that while I slept the snipers had been captured, or at least that all the pieces had come together and there was a specific lookout issued. But there was nothing new to report.

As I drove south, I listened to both the police radio and the car radio. The police radio sounded nothing but normal—troopers were active, making traffic stops. The difference was that there were a lot more cruisers on the road, and they were unusually active for so early in the morning, well before sunrise. Troopers were calling out every traffic stop, and other troopers were responding as backup. I felt anxious listening to the police radio. I couldn't help fearing that some trooper, deputy, or county officer had stumbled upon the Caprice and paid the ultimate price for the effort. The vast majority of cops out there working the street didn't have the same level of information and knowledge that I had, and that gnawed at me. What if one of my brothers or sisters got killed because they didn't know that the focus of the investigation was turning toward tracking down a blue Caprice? Because of all the leaks, I understood that information about this Caprice was being kept close to the vest. And if this news got out prematurely, the press would be all over it, and we would lose any advantage the narrowing of the focus had gained us. But still I didn't like it. Cops who needed to know this detail may not know it. They were still focusing on the damn white van.

I scanned through the stations on the car radio, but there was nothing new on any of the news channels. Instead, I was hearing the same repeated drivel from so-called experts as to who the killers were likely to be. They were also spewing out theories about what the police were probably doing to further this investigation, or should be doing. One damn thing I was sure of. If I ever needed an idea about what I should do next, all I had to do was turn on the radio or TV, and some expert would tell me what the hell I should be doing.

The media hadn't picked up on the fact that we were narrowing our field and were beginning to look for specific individuals. It amazed me to realize that when the feds really wanted to keep something under their hat, they could. Since the first letter was leaked within a few hours, I was surprised that the identities of the persons of interest hadn't been leaked to the press. There were all kinds of stories and speculation being floated in the media, but no mention of the facts. I wanted to believe that the press were finally on board and were willing to withhold information in the best interests of doing their part to help us get these guys. But more likely the leaker was getting nervous that he or she would be discovered. Or maybe the leaker had realized that the leaks could have contributed to some of the shootings and was now keeping quiet because of a belated case of morals. Whatever the reason, it was a positive.

As I made my way to the operations center, I called Lieutenant Chase of the Frederick City Police Department and brought him up to speed. I told him about the Caprice but let him know it still wasn't verified. "We're waiting to hear back from other investigative teams from across the country," I said. "We're starting to focus on the Caprice, but we still can't discount the possibility of the white van or truck, since it kept coming up as being seen at just about all of the shootings. My gut tells me these bastards are in the Caprice and the van is nothing but bullshit, but I just can't completely discount it yet."

"Dave," said Chase, ever the professional, "can I pass what you told me on to the chief? I'm also worried about one of our cops blindly running into these guys."

"Do what you need to do to keep your cops safe," I said. "This can't get to the press until the timing is right, but I *know* these bastards are lying low in our community. I just know it."

"I think these guys are up here too," he said. "It makes too much sense for them not to be. Anyway, I'll pass the word personally, and there will be nothing put out over the radio about any of this. But I'll make sure our cops at least know about the damn Caprice."

"This will be over soon, Tom," I said. "I can feel it. And when it ends, it'll end in a gunfight."

The concern was thick in his response. "Stay safe, buddy. You're probably right. This may not end well. We just have to make sure that in the end the cops win this fight."

"We'll win," I said. "But at what cost?"

I hung up the phone and continued south toward the operations center, wondering what this day was going to bring.

When an investigation finally gets to the stage of identifying a person or persons of interest, when should the police go public with that information? This is a question that every cop who has ever worked a major crime has wrestled with. It's not always the right decision to go public, and often more things can go wrong once information has been released. An innocent person can be ruined for life, for example, as in the case of the Olympic bombing in Atlanta. The suspect whose name and face were plastered all over the press turned out to be innocent, but the police couldn't take back the damage that had been done. On the other hand, if the name and description of a suspect aren't released quickly enough, we run the risk of more citizens becoming victims. The higher the profile of the case, the greater the conundrum. This sniper case was now all over the news, every day, worldwide.

By going public, there's a real risk that we'll give the bad guys helpful information. Sometimes it's better to just let them stay comfortable and unaware. If we were to put out a BOLO and it went public—a given, since the media were listening to police radio traffic—the killers would likely dump their car and steal something else. They could just jump from vehicle to vehicle until they simply vanished. That's what I would have done, and I was surprised that they hadn't been doing this all along. We had been monitoring stolen car reports from the entire region since the shooting started, but it was evident through our analysis that they were still using the Caprice. Once we caught them, it would become clear why they didn't want to abandon their ride. But this key to their crimes was also sloppy on their part, giving us a chance to track down the car with them in it.

For the past three weeks all our efforts had been toward identifying a suspect. But now that we had both suspects and a suspect vehicle, we shifted gears. The new goal was to find where the suspects were hiding, and our team agreed that the best place to start was with the two killers' electronic footprint. The Caprice had to have gas. It had to be moving around, which meant there was a trail out there somewhere. If we could find where they had been, it might help us predict where they might go.

In 2002 there still weren't a lot of traffic cameras around the metropolitan area, but there were a few. There were also plenty of other security cameras attached to government buildings and shopping malls. Security camera footage is only as good as the camera and the recording medium it uses. The old VHS tapes were of such poor quality that they were almost useless. By the time of the sniper case, the newer digital systems were showing up here and there, and they provided much cleaner images. The problem was (and continues to be to this day) a matter of money and attitude. Private companies hate to pay for security because it comes directly out of the bottom line and contributes nothing to profit. But there are insurance benefits to having security cameras, so even small businesses had cameras just like the big-box retail stores and corporate offices did. Mostly, though, they recorded on VHS. In order to save money, VHS tapes were used, then copied over multiple times. The more they were copied over, the worse the quality became, until all you could see were shadows. Since nobody ever looked at these tapes until they were needed, most managers had no idea that their cameras and video recording equipment were useless.

Now that we knew the suspects were in possession of at least one stolen credit card, we instructed the credit card company to activate the card and attach a flag. We would be notified immediately if they attempted to use it. We were looking at all parking tickets and tollbooth violations that had been issued throughout the region. The idea was to cast a large enough net covering a wide enough range of data and information. If these guys had popped up anywhere, or were *going* to pop up anywhere in the immediate future, we would know when and where as quickly as possible. I instructed our group to focus our intelligence searches to the north of the killers' preferred hunting ground; that, I strongly believed, was where we were going to find them.

By the evening of October 23, all the verifiable information concerning Muhammad, Malvo, and the blue Caprice had been verified. We issued flyers with their pictures, along with the plate and tag number information. We found a picture of an old Caprice similar to what we knew they were driving, and that was also placed on the wanted flyer. It was decision time for us. We were done playing defense. It was time to go on the hunt.

27

October 23, 8 p.m. I walked into the conference area and break room one floor down from the intelligence team area. As I entered, I quickly realized that I was the highest-ranking trooper in the room. It was getting later into the evening, and the majority of our top brass had gone home out of sheer exhaustion. Rank is relative, depending on the police agency. My rank of lieutenant in intelligence was equal to the rank of captain or major in other departments. It all depended on your responsibility. A state police lieutenant is commissioned by the governor and is considered a commander. Most troopers rarely have to deal with anybody of a higher rank. To a working trooper, the lieutenant is the old man and is to be respected and feared. But at the joint operations center there were usually several lieutenants and a captain or major hanging around, so I was a little surprised that I outranked everyone in the room. I wasn't concerned about it—I knew that my captain, major, and the colonel had full faith in me. Commanders who can't cut it are quickly removed from the field and stashed in nonoperational functions. I knew Captain McAndrew was still working, but he was somewhere else. Anyway, I walked in and plopped my tired ass into one of the folding chairs.

In front of me, eighteen experienced investigators along with the task force leadership and top agents from the FBI and ATF were arguing. Should they release the flyers and the suspect information to all the police units out on the street? If they did, would that give the suspects time to dump their car? Once lookouts were broadcast over the police channels, the news media would pick up on it immediately. Then the media frenzy would hit. Regularly scheduled programming would be interrupted. There would be no way of stopping the suspects from hearing it.

I had worked with these agencies in the past. What I was hearing, in my opinion, was more interagency jealousy. Each group had already made a partial release to their own agents, and they had agents in the field looking for the Caprice, and each agency was hoping to be the one to catch the big fish. After three weeks of working together as a combined team at levels never before seen in law enforcement, the whole thing was breaking down because it was nearly time for the big we-got-'em press release, and each federal agency wanted to be the one that got them. They all wanted to be the ones leading Muhammad and Malvo in the "perp walk" for the TV cameras.

Who the hell cares who puts the cuffs on the bastards? The point was to capture them and stop the killings. Every one of us wanted this to end. We wanted to be able to go home, have dinner with our families, watch some TV, play with the dog, and above all else get some sleep. As I sat there listening to this inane back and forth, I couldn't get over how *stupid* this was becoming. We had worked together so well over the past three weeks, and I'd be damned if it was going to fall apart over who got to do the perp walk. The anger welled up inside of me, and I just lost it.

"Who the hell is going to pay for the trooper's funeral?" I blurted out. "We have all this information about the car and the suspects, and we're not sharing it with them? What happens if some trooper or officer out there stops the Caprice on what they think is a routine traffic stop and they get their fucking head blown off?" I wasn't directing my comments to anybody in particular. I was tired and frustrated, and could not believe that while our entire region was holding its breath in fear, and the rest of the country was afraid that this would start happening in *their* neighborhoods, here we were like a bunch of five-year-olds arguing over who gets the last damn cupcake.

If looks could kill, I would've been taking an immediate dirt nap. More than one of the lead agents in that room shot me one of those "who the hell do you think you are" looks. I was too tired and pissed off to care. I stepped out of the room and exhaled. Then I called state police headquarters and was promptly connected to

Colonel Mitchell. I briefed him on what was happening. He was less than pleased. Then he gave me a direct order. I was to fax a flyer to headquarters to be immediately broadcast to all state police units in Maryland. He wanted every police car in the state to have the information *right now*. I was told to mass-produce the flyers and get them distributed as quickly as possible. He also told me to let the task force know that these were my orders, and if anybody had any problems with them they could contact him directly. He also told me to get the flyers over to the Rockville Barrack to have them assist in the distribution.

Finally, he said this would be a good time for me to get the hell out of the joint operations center. "Dave," he said, "you were okay right up to the part when you asked them which one of them was going to pay for the funeral." He chuckled. "I'm sure you pissed off some big-time federal egos, but that's my boy. I can get away with that shit, a lieutenant can't." There it was—I had direct orders from the boss. For the first time in a long time I felt like I had a mission, something I could personally do that would contribute to the overall mission at hand.

Colonel Mitchell's language was a little more colorful than what I just described, but the point was that he and I were clearly on the same page. And since he was the boss, I had no problem seeing to it that those orders were carried out. The bottom line was this: although we were all working together on this thing, I didn't work for the FBI or ATF. I worked for the Maryland State Police.

I went back to the conference room and announced what my orders were and then promptly left the room, leaving some angry agents in my wake. I didn't give a rat's ass what they thought. I had my orders, and I was damn well going to carry them out.

I grabbed a handful of flyers, jumped into car 662, and headed out to the Rockville Barrack. On the way I called the state police duty officer in our Pikesville headquarters and relayed my orders. I told him I would be faxing them a copy of the flyer from the Rockville Barrack in a few minutes.

28

It was now about 10:30 p.m. The initial flyers had been distributed. Before going home, I called the Frederick Barrack duty officer and spoke to Sergeant Hundertmark, whom I had known for many years. He was a highly respected sergeant who took good care of the troopers under his command. I also knew that whatever I asked him to do would be done immediately and without question. He was the kind of sergeant that I had been lucky enough to work for as a young trooper. He knew what he was doing, stood behind his troopers, knew how to lead, and, most important, gave a damn. He understood that what we do matters.

I told him I was about to start driving north toward Frederick carrying one hundred flyers, and asked that he have a trooper meet me around the Francis Scott Key Mall, just off I-270, so I could pass them along for further distribution. The mall was in an area known as Evergreen Point, and I lived just a few minutes' drive from there. I instructed Hundertmark to make sure additional flyers were made and sent to all the barracks north and west. I also wanted him to make sure the Frederick County sheriff's department got copies for all their deputies, and that copies were also distributed to the Frederick City Police Department. I still had it in the back of my mind that these guys were staying in Frederick County.

My next call was to my old friend Lieutenant Chase from

Frederick City. I told him about the information and the flyer, and let him know that I was on my way north to make sure that everybody had a copy. I repeated my thought that the killers were in the Frederick area somewhere. "Make sure your cops are on their toes, Tom. I know these bastards are hiding in plain sight in our backyard."

"I'll make sure our guys are looking behind every building, dumpster, and rock in Frederick," he said. "If these fuckers are up here, we'll find them."

"Tell the boys to take zero chances and to do whatever they need to do to get home in one piece to their families. If that means shoot first, then kill the bastards on the spot."

There really was no need for further discussion or conversation. We knew what was needed, and we both knew the killers were in our area. It made sense to both of us old cops. I could feel it in my bones.

I pulled out of the Rockville Barrack and headed north to Frederick County. It was about a thirty-mile ride to the Francis Scott Key Mall exit where I was to meet the Frederick Barrack trooper. I was in car 662, ironically an unmarked blue Chevrolet Caprice that had a lot of wear and tear. It was fast approaching two hundred thousand miles. My Caprice wasn't as dark a blue as the one we were looking for, but the coincidence was a little creepy. Their car represented evil and terror, mine represented justice.

I had driven about five miles up I-270 when I heard the first BOLO going out over the Rockville Barrack channel to all cars. I knew this pissed off the FBI command, but they just needed to get over it. As I came close to crossing into Frederick County, I switched the police radio to the Frederick Barrack channel and announced my presence in the county—something we were required to do. "Car 662 Frederick, I am 10-8 [in service] in the county."

There were a few seconds of radio static, then the barrack police communications officer acknowledged my message. "Car 662, be advised that car B-12 [Frederick Barrack cars were assigned the letter B followed by a numerical identifier] will be waiting in the Sears parking lot," she said.

"Copy that," I responded, and replaced the radio mike.

In less than thirty seconds, the radio came alive again. This time, it was Sergeant Hundertmark speaking. "Frederick car 662, can you switch over to the secure channel and contact me immediately?"

Something was up. Something serious. Sergeant Hundertmark had been around the Maryland State Police for a long time. He had experienced plenty in his career, and he wasn't one for theatrics or for inappropriate use of secure lines; he wouldn't ask me to go to the secure channel to ask how Jean and the kids were doing.

I switched over to channel one. The channel wasn't totally secure but was a frequency that had never been publicly assigned. Few people would have known to be listening to it on scanners. It was also unlikely that anybody from the press would be listening to channel one in Frederick County. After all, they were all concentrating on Montgomery County south.

"Car 662 Frederick. Go ahead on channel one."

Hundertmark immediately responded. "Car 662, we just received a cell phone call from a citizen in the westbound rest area on I-70. The caller advised that there is a Caprice in the rest area parking lot, and then repeated the tag that we had put out over the air."

I think my heart stopped beating for a millisecond before the adrenaline started rushing in. After so many days of not knowing, of searching, often without a trace of a clue, here was a possible sighting.

"Sergeant, how many troopers do you have at your disposal?" I asked.

"I have two right now, but I can get one or two more out of Hagerstown."

Not exactly the cavalry, I thought. I sucked in my breath. "Send everybody you've got. Have them meet me at the entrance to the rest area. Notify the MSP command staff—I'll handle notifying the JOC. And tell them to respond silent. I don't want to risk alerting these guys."

"Just so you know," Hundertmark said, "I put out the first broadcast and BOLO for the Caprice less than five minutes before this call came in."

No sleep for me tonight either. But unlike last night, this night was about to get a hell of a lot more interesting.

29

October 23, 10:30 p.m. There were too many things racing through my mind all at once. I had to get there before that car took off. I just had to. And I didn't want any more information going over the air than was necessary. I called the barrack on my cell phone and spoke directly to Sergeant Hundertmark.

I had to make sure we had a witness in case the killers slipped by us. I asked Hundertmark if he still had contact with the witness.

"I do, yes."

"Get his cell phone number and find out all you can about what he saw. Make sure the caller is safe, and find out if he saw anybody in or around the car. Oh, and find out how many people and vehicles this guy estimates are in the rest area. Who's moving around the area?" My mind was going faster than my ability to give instructions to Hundertmark.

"And sergeant?"

"Yes?"

I hesitated. Surely it was the right car, but we had to be sure. "Can you have the caller recheck the tag number and description of the car? Tell him to do that only if it's safe to do so."

I gave Hundertmark my cell phone number. "Use the Frederick Barrack resources. Set up a conference call with the witness. I want to be able to speak directly with the caller when I get on the scene." I was also thinking the barrack would be able to monitor what was being said so that nothing would be missed.

Before I hung up, I asked Hundertmark to contact the MSP hangar at the Frederick airport and make sure that the helicopter Trooper 3 was fueled and ready upon my call, should we need aerial support or to medivac any of my troopers if this went bad.

"I'll take care of it," he said.

The one thing that could be to my advantage this night was that these guys had been found on my home turf. They would have to face some of the best troopers the Maryland State Police had.

At the time, the MSP were using Nextel cell phones with direct connect. Not all troopers had them—only command staff and troopers assigned to certain divisions and commands that needed "private and immediate communications." Nearly all the road troopers had bought their own personal cell phones and used them for work, because the state police didn't have the budget to provide everyone with a phone. The Intelligence Division had need for private and immediate communications, so we had been issued phones.

As I drove car 662 toward the rest area, I dialed Captain

McAndrew on the Nextel. A very tired voice answered. I contained my excitement, but just barely. "Captain, it's Reichenbaugh. We have a reported sighting of the sniper suspects in the I-70 westbound rest area in Frederick County. I'm headed there now and should arrive in a few minutes."

Silence. Then his voice became more animated. "Got it. What are the orders so far?"

I told him what orders I had issued to Sergeant Hundertmark. "I think we've got the situation under control," I said. "Would you pass the info to the JOC? I don't have time to play a thousand questions with them. I'm kind of busy driving like a bat out of hell. Besides, I'm about the last bastard that pack of morons wants to hear from."

"Something I should know?" he asked.

"I'm sure you'll hear about it later, but nothing to worry about right now."

McAndrew sounded energized. "You got it," he said.

"Good. Once I'm on the scene, I'll set up car 662 as the command and control vehicle. Have all other cars disable their repeater systems so that all repeater needs for the handheld radios will run through me."

"I'll take care of it." I knew he would. McAndrew, like all troopers who have worked in the trenches together, always had my back. One less thing I would have to worry about as this unfolded.

I was taking a chance with the repeater system. If another car coming into the area with a repeater system—which takes a weak received signal and rebroadcasts it stronger—was on another channel, it could unintentionally take over the repeater function, and all the cars would lose communication with the command car, causing an unintentional communication blackout. I had fallen victim to this in other situations, and I *really* didn't want to experience it now. By having the others disable their systems, we could avoid an accidental communications blackout. It sure as hell wasn't an ideal situation, but it was what I had to work with. So the radio system I had would have to do.

When the first call from Sergeant Hundertmark had come, I was more than forty miles from the rest area. Having worked most of my career in Frederick County, I knew that rest area well. I had patrolled it many times during my uniformed days, and had set up more than one undercover drug deal there because it was an easy area to control. One way in, one way out. Plus, it was a public area where people were always coming and going, so it was easy to set up a surveillance team to monitor and record the drug buys. The problem was, it was public access. Hopefully we would get lucky now and there wouldn't be a ton of people there at this time of night.

If the snipers had decided to lie low in this rest area, they had made a huge mistake: they had boxed themselves in. All we had to do was shut both the entrance ramp and exit ramp before they realized it.

This particular rest area is located a few miles west of Myersville on top of Old South Mountain, less than two hundred yards from the Washington County line. South Mountain had been the scene of numerous historic events stretching back to before the Revolutionary War. During the French and Indian War campaigns, General Braddock, accompanied by a young George Washington, had traveled in, around, and over a pass near where I-70 cuts over the mountain. The Civil War battle of South Mountain happened here, and the mountain also served as observation posts during the fighting at Antietam. In addition, General Lee had marched the Army of Northern Virginia on the west side of the mountain to shield his movements from the Union Army as he plunged deep into Pennsylvania on his way to the showdown at Gettysburg. Once again, this spot was going to be thrust into American history, only this time a modern-day showdown between law enforcement and two serial killers who would come to be known as the Beltway snipers.

As I was clocking over 110 miles per hour toward that rest area, I was determined not to let it become another battleground. If this turned out to be the snipers in the rest area, I wanted all my troopers to go home in one piece to their families and loved ones. That was my responsibility. I had never lost a trooper under my command, and I was damn well resolved not to let that happen now. The fate of the two killers would likely be their choice, but we were going to do our best to bring them to justice with little or no force or violence.

Plus, we didn't want to let them slip through our fingers or make them martyrs for some perverse cause they may have thought themselves part of. We didn't want to fuel some other nutbag's desire to commit some future heinous act of violence. I was determined to make this nothing more than a call to justice for a couple of scumbag bushwhackers.

I laid my right foot hard on the accelerator, pressing it to the floor. The big engine roared, and I could feel myself being pressed back into the seat as the roller accelerated. Car 662 had a lot of miles on it, but I knew it wouldn't fail and would give me every ounce of power it had. The grille lights flashed red and blue, and the portable blue strobe I had thrown up on the dash reflected off the guardrails. There was no need for a siren because there was really nobody else on the road. I was more than thirty-five miles from the rest area, so I wasn't concerned that the killers would see or hear me coming. I had been trained to drive fast in pursuit. All my training and years of experience were kicking in, and the words of Corporal Cameron were in my ear from more than twenty years before: "Don't fuck this up, son. If you don't get there alive or you kill somebody else trying to get there you'll be of no use to the agency, or to anybody depending on you to save their asses."

I began to think about what I was racing toward. I was likely going to be the senior trooper, and the highest-ranking one, on the scene. This entire incident was about to become my total responsibility. It should have made me nervous, but it didn't. I felt well prepared. I knew the incident command structure that had been adopted by all police agencies and emergency management agencies throughout the country—post-9/11, it had been drilled into all of us on a more detailed basis. I was cocky, arrogant, determined, well trained, experienced, and a Maryland state trooper, Maryland's finest. I was in my element. Failure never entered my mind.

30

While this rest area was going to cause me some logistical problems, it also had some features that I intended to use to our full advantage. It was a typical rest area layout, with an exit ramp off I-70 that funneled vehicle traffic to the right into a parking and picnic area; large trucks, buses, and campers stayed straight to a much larger parking area. Situated between the two parking areas was a building with restroom facilities and a small tourist information center. There were several vending machines as well.

The building and parking lots had been carved out of the uneven, rocky terrain. Cell phones hadn't yet become staples, so there was still a bank of five or six public pay telephones lining the sidewalk in front of the restroom facility.

A large embankment protected the rest area from cars flying off the interstate into the truck parking lot; it also blocked any view of the rest area from the interstate. Over the years, that embankment had grown over with mature trees and thick underbrush. The rest area itself was wooded, the building and parking lots surrounded by very large oaks. Sparse grass grew under the heavy tree canopy. Dispersed along the walkway from the truck lot were picnic tables. On the opposite side of the car parking lot was a small grassy area less than thirty yards wide with more picnic tables and a few grills. Behind that were more trees and thick underbrush on rocky terrain. The entire area was poorly lit, with tall streetlights that couldn't cut through the foliage well; the lighting was spotted, diffused, and dim to dark in areas. All of this mattered. We had to be able to anticipate the killers' moves while knowing what our logistical position would be at all times.

There was a nip in the late-October air. I hoped the chill would help keep the snipers in their car. The foliage was still full, for the most part, and the leaves on the trees had just begun to take on their fall colors.

My advantage was my familiarity with the area. The troopers responding with me were also going to be well aware of the topography. I had hunted that mountain and hiked all over it over the years. I wasn't concerned with the snipers' making an escape on foot through the woods. The terrain was dark and rocky—not a good place to be stumbling around trying to flee the police. That would also be to our advantage. If they tried to escape on foot, they would face maybe four miles in the dark over rocks and

Crime scene photo of the second written communication from the snipers, found in the woods behind a Ponderosa Steak House in Ashland, Virginia, again located just off 1-95, where on October 19 at 7:19 p.m. Jeffrey Hopper was shot in the parking lot as he and his wife exited the restaurant. The note was found in a plastic bag tacked to a tree from where the snipers took their shot.

Crime scene photo of spent shell casing of the .223-caliber bullet used to shoot Hopper. The snipers were beginning to get sloppy and leave behind valuable evidence.

The cover page of the letter left for the police to find at the Ponderosa shooting of October 19.

The first page of the letter to police, taunting them and boasting about the snipers' superior skills.

For you mr. Police
" Call me God"

Do not release to the Press.

"For you Mr. Police
"Call me God."

Do not release to the press.
We have tried to contact you to start negotiation, But the incompetence of your forces in
(i) Mongomery Police "Officer Derick" at 240 - 773 - 5000 Friday.
(ii) Rockville Police Dept "female officer" at 301 -309- 3100.
(iii) Task force "FBI" " female" at 1888-324-9800 (four times)
(iv) Priest at ashland.
(v) an Washington DC. at 202 -898-7900
These people took of calls for a Hoax or Joke ,so your failure to respond has cost you five lives.

'y ∠.

more important than catching us now, then you will accept our demand which are non-nego-tiable.

(i) You will place ten million dollar in Bank of america. account no. 4024-0046-2875-9173.
Pin no. 9595.
Activation date 08/01/01/
Exp. date 09/04.
Name: Jill Lynn Farell.
member since 1974.
Platinum Visa Account.
We will have unlimited ~~withdra~~ withdrawl at any atm world-wide.
You will activate the bank account, credit card, and Pin number.

The second page of the sniper letter to the police, containing their demand for money and the means to get the money to them. This letter and the information contained in it would prove valuable in ultimately identifying the snipers.

(ASHLAND, VA)
Ponderosa Buffet tel #. 798-9205
6:00 am Sunday morning.
You have until 9:00 a.m Monday morning to complete transaction.
" Try to catch us withdrawing at least you will have less body bags."
(BuT)
(i) If trying to catch us now more important then prepare you body bags.
If we give you our word that is what takes place "Word is Bond!"

P.S. your children are not safe anywhere at any time.

The third page of the sniper letter to the police left at the crime scene of the Ponderosa shooting. The third page was a clear warning to the police as to what would happen if the snipers' demands were not met.

Crime scene photo from the snipers' hiding place, toward the Ponderosa parking lot where Hopper was shot as he and his wife came out of the restaurant.

LEFT Crime scene photo of a boot print left behind by the snipers in the woods behind the Ponderosa Steak House in Ashland, Virginia, on October 19.

RIGHT Photo of a fingerprint that was found on a magazine recovered from the scene of a murder at a convenience store in Alabama in September 2002. The small smudge was used to identify Lee Malvo and connect him to the Beltway sniper shootings.

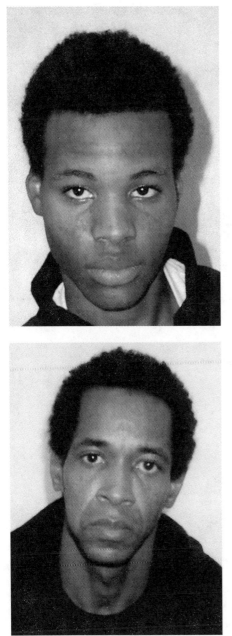

Mug shot of teenage killer
Lee Boyd Malvo.

Mug shot of the
mastermind and killer
John Allen Muhammad.

Crime scene photo from October 22, when at 5:56 a.m. Conrad Johnson was shot and killed by the snipers in Silver Spring, Maryland, as he prepared his Ride-On Bus for his daily route. Police found another note in a plastic bag in the woods near the bus.

The first page of the letter found in the woods at the scene where Conrad Johnson was shot. The letter, covered with red stars, is directed at the police. "Can you hear us now!" The snipers were angry that their demands had not been met.

The blue Chevrolet Caprice that was used by the snipers as a mobile sniper's nest. This is a photo as the car appears today at the National Law Enforcement Museum.

Crime scene photo of the blue Caprice where it was found parked at the Myersville rest area off Interstate 70 in Frederick County, Maryland, on October 23. The snipers had been captured, and a search-and-seizure warrant for the car was being prepared. The author is in the foreground.

The exit ramp coming out of the westbound rest area on top of South Mountain on I-70, appearing much as it did the night the snipers were captured. The author's police car, along with Trooper Dwayne Smith's police car, would have been in the foreground, in front of the truck blocking the exit.

The third parking spot from the right is where the snipers had parked the night they were captured. The car was backed into the parking space. The night the snipers were captured, the tree canopy was much heavier. The tree line has been cut back since the sniper case.

The heavily forested embankment that separated the rest area from the interstate. The snipers could not see out of the rest area from where they were, and the police could not see in.

View from inside the rest area looking out toward the exit ramp where the author had set up his command. The author used exiting tractor trailers to assist in blocking the ramp, much as they appear in this photo.

Crime scene photo of the blue Caprice within a few minutes of the suspects being forcibly removed from the car.

View of the rear of the sniper car as it would have appeared while it was being used. The trunk would have been slightly open for the rifle's optical sights, while the barrel would have protruded from the notch cut into the trunk above the license plate. The shooter would have been prone and concealed inside the trunk, with the back seat pulled down to allow access. Note the crime-scene evidence tape still on the trunk lid. Exhibits courtesy National Law Enforcement Museum. Photo by the author.

Crime scene photo of the .223-caliber Bushmaster rifle used by the snipers as it was found behind the back seat of the Caprice.

The author demonstrating how the rifle's barrel was poked out through the notch while in use. Note how the inside of the trunk lid was painted a matching blue to help conceal the slightly opened trunk while the snipers lined up their target and fired the rifle. Exhibits courtesy National Law Enforcement Museum. Photo by Jean Reichenbaugh.

Display of the sniper rifle and other firearms and evidence recovered from the Caprice. All evidence is now in the possession of the museum. Exhibits courtesy National Law Enforcement Museum. Photo by the author.

Wall of evidence, including crime scene photo documents and reports generated by the Beltway sniper investigation, collected and preserved by the National Law Enforcement Museum. Exhibits courtesy National Law Enforcement Museum. Photo by the author.

The blue Caprice used by the snipers, as it appears today at the National Law Enforcement Museum, is preserved in the same state in which the author last saw it in the rest area. For the author, being in the presence of this car is a surreal experience that immediately brings back the horror created by the two killers who used it. Exhibits courtesy National Law Enforcement Museum. Photo by the author.

through briars and underbrush before they came to any roads. They weren't from around here; even if they did make a run for it, they wouldn't know where they were and would have to stick to roads. Those we would be able to cover, and eventually flood with police cars, K-9 patrol dogs, and bloodhounds that would easily track them down. Also, the cold air provided perfect conditions for our FLIR (forward-looking infrared) mounted on Trooper 3 back at the airport. And the fact that the highway couldn't be seen from inside the rest area meant we could surround the killers without their being aware of it.

But much of this was also to our disadvantage. If they couldn't see us, we couldn't see them; that would make it hard to know exactly what was happening in the rest area. Also, the poor lighting contributed to the problem. We had no night-vision equipment and no idea if they did. Since they had already shot at and hit a target using the rifle at night, I made the safe assumption that they could very well have night-vision equipment at their disposal. We also knew we were outgunned. They were in possession of at least one sniper rifle and had demonstrated time and again that they had the willingness and the ability to shoot, hit their target, and take a human life. If cornered, we could expect no less than a shootout.

We were armed with .40-caliber pistols. A few of us had shotguns that we could either load with buckshot or rifled slugs. Since I was a lieutenant in a nonuniformed investigative function, I didn't have a shotgun assigned to me. The state police had a limited supply of Remington 870 shotguns, and they had been reserved for the road troopers.

In any case, a shotgun—even if loaded with rifled slugs— wouldn't be a match for a sniper rifle. The snipers would be able to shoot at us and penetrate our ballistic vests before we could get anywhere near range to fight back. It was critical to improve our odds, so we would compensate for that disadvantage with the element of surprise.

There were other factors to consider, too. There likely would be other cars and tractor trailers in that rest area, but how many? I was concerned about creating a hostage barricade situation, in which the snipers took a motorist or sleeping driver hostage. If we had to engage the snipers immediately, we would do it in order to prevent that from happening. We also wanted to keep them from gaining access to a large vehicle, such as a tractor trailer. That could create real problems for us if this turned into a chase. The last thing we wanted was a high-speed gunfight on an interstate highway, which would dramatically increase the possibility of loss of life. Bottom line: If we were going to maintain control of this situation as it unfolded, we had to contain them in the rest area.

As I drove the thirty-five-plus miles, I noticed there still wasn't much traffic. I passed a few cars and trucks as I went westbound and saw just a few trucks traveling east. That was a good sign. Fewer vehicles meant we could devote more police resources to the situation at hand, as opposed to needing to use them to keep the public back. Also, the radio silence was an advantage. The quieter we could be, the more time I would have to set a perimeter without the press converging on the scene. The longer we could delay the story getting out, the better our odds of preserving the scene. It was an unfortunate distraction that I had to think about the press as well as the bad guys, but it was a necessity. If the media wasn't managed properly, this would very quickly turn into an uncontrollable media circus.

By the time I made it to Myersville, about three miles east of the rest area, the word was getting out. I received a phone call from Special Agent Bruce McCauley at the Secret Service. Agent

McCauley was stationed at nearby Fort Detrick and was responsible for presidential protection at Camp David, also located on South Mountain, about twenty miles farther north. McCauley and I had worked together on some of the Secret Service's counterfeit cases in and around the state. Plus, as part of the state police duties, I routinely assisted the Service when the sitting president was spending time at Camp David and wanted to step out in the county for dinner or recreation.

McCauley and I discussed my concern about press coverage, and about the airspace around the rest area. "The worst thing that could happen," I said, "was a media helicopter hovering overhead and waking these guys up."

"You thinking hostage situation?"

"That or a shootout—either one isn't good. And the last thing I need to worry about right now is the media fucking this up for me."

"Not a problem," McCauley said. "I'll have the Service declare the entire region a no-fly zone. I'll call back when it's done."

He called back just as I reached the rest area entrance ramp— the no-fly zone was in place. One thing no licensed pilot would do was to cross the Secret Service with a secured airspace violation. That brought jail time and permanent grounding.

At the entrance ramp I saw two marked MSP rollers parked across the roadway to prevent anybody from entering. A third, marked K-9 car was pulling up just as I arrived. I came to a stop behind them and checked in with the barrack duty officer.

"Any updates from our witness?"

"I still have him on the phone," Sergeant Hundertmark said. "Nothing's changed. He and another person are parked in the truck lot." It was the rest area caretaker who had spotted the blue Caprice; he had apparently made contact with another person in the truck lot, a Mr. Donovan, who was parked in a small work van. Donovan had a cell phone, which they had used to contact the state police barrack. They were now both inside the work van. "They have a good view of the suspect vehicle," the sergeant said. "They feel they're safe for now. They are confirming the tag number and the description of the vehicle."

We took a quick look around. Because of the layout of the rest area and the heavy woods around it, there wasn't much we could see from where we were. The real problem was that we couldn't see the target vehicle. On the other hand, if they were in the car, then they couldn't see us, either. If they were smart enough to have a lookout in the woods watching the end of the ramp, then we were sitting ducks. But since nobody had tried to kill us yet, we were hoping for the best, but prepared for the worst. There were two other cars parked in the lot, one of which belonged to the caretaker who was now inside Mr. Donovan's van in the truck lot. The rest area also contained at least a dozen parked tractor trailers along with their sleeping drivers.

"They've seen no one in or around the Caprice," the sergeant said. "The area's been quiet. No movement by anyone."

"Okay," I said. "Keep the caller on the line. I'll speak with him as soon as I have the perimeter secured."

31

Once again, luck was on my side. One of the troopers waiting for my arrival was Trooper First Class Rob Draskovic. Drak and I had worked together on the Frederick County Narcotics Task Force for many years, and we knew each other well. It was great to see the big man standing there as I pulled up. TFC Draskovic was one of the largest people I had ever seen. At over six-six and in the neighborhood of 265 to 280 pounds, Drak was an intimidating presence. He was a nice guy, but he didn't need to say a word to intimidate someone.

I knew exactly what to expect from Drak, and he knew what to expect from me. We had served many search-and-seizure warrants together. He'd had the same training that I'd had, working with the STATE teams, and the two of us had come face to face with armed drug dealers on more than one occasion. If I'd had an opportunity to pick a trooper to face the snipers with me, Drak would have been at the top of my list. The other trooper waiting there was Trooper First Class Chris Paschal. I knew that TFC Paschal was also an outstanding, highly experienced trooper, and he would have easily been my second choice. The trooper in the K-9 car was Corporal Rich Poffenberger, another experienced hand. He had his German shepherd partner with him in the back seat. "I just pulled up to Drak a few seconds before you got here," said Rich, leaning out the window. Rich was another trooper that was not to be fucked with. Armed with a big smile, a dry sense of humor, and a kick-ass dog, he wouldn't blink at anything that was about to happen. Another big man that I was damn glad was here and was on my side.

"Yeah, Dave, I got here about five minutes ago," Drak said. "I got the ramp blocked and did a sneak-and-peek foot recon through the woods."

"And?" I asked.

"Confirmed. It's the Caprice. I used binoculars, but didn't see anyone in or around the car. The car is to the right in the car parking area, third or fourth space in. They backed it in. The trunk is facing the woods."

If I were in their shoes I would have also backed into a parking space. That would give me an opportunity for a quick getaway. If there was any doubt left, it was gone now. These guys were the killers. They were constantly aware of their tactical situation. That also made them that much more dangerous and formidable.

I got on the radio. "Sergeant, is our caller still on the line?"

"He is. He's waiting for your call. He's still with the other person, still in a safe place."

Nothing had changed since my last update. Good.

Drak, Chris, Rich, and I took a few minutes and evaluated the tactical situation we were facing. Our biggest concern: not having any idea where the snipers were, or even if they were in the rest area. It was entirely possible that they had heard about the lookout for their car and simply walked away from the rest area or carjacked another motorist.

It was now after 11 p.m., though, and I suspected they were sleeping in the car. But putting myself in their position, I would have slept in shifts. I would have had one of us watch from somewhere in the woods with the sniper rifle while the partner slept. They had already used a wooded area in several of the shootings, so it wouldn't have been out of character for them to do that. If that were the case, and if we tried to either sneak in and take them or use a full-on lights-and-siren raid, we might very well walk into an ambush. While we would be able to pin the car in the parking spot, our sidearms and the one shotgun we had among us weren't going to be a match for a sniper rifle with night sights or a laser sight. Hell, if they did have one of them on watch while the other one slept, we might well be in their rifle sights as we stood there talking.

But my gut told me otherwise. I felt that we had the element of surprise on our side, but we still needed to consider all options. If it were me, I would have been watching the entrance ramp to the rest area but would have stayed close enough to the car to get back and peel out before the exit was blocked. Anyway, there was a chance they hadn't seen us. Maybe they were just a couple of lucky dumbasses and I was giving them way too much credit. If they were watching the ramp and had already seen Drak, they would have opened up on him, or they would have slipped out of the rest area. But nothing. Our caller was continuing to relay to us that there was no movement.

Another possibility: If they happened to be in the restroom and we secured their car without them in it, we could easily create a hostage barricade situation. Their only option would be to flee and try to commandeer one of the trucks or any of the other cars with people in them. With the number of shootings and killings these two guys had been involved with over the span of the last three weeks, a hostage situation was the last thing I wanted to see happen. It always came back to that. The body count was already way too high.

The risk of the four of us trying to take them was unacceptable—too unpredictable. "Boys," I said, "no matter what happens tonight, we go home alive, and they don't get out of this rest area. This case ends tonight."

We looked at one another. Game time.

"Drak, keep the entrance ramp secured. No one comes in or goes out. Rich, get into the median strip and turn your dog loose on anybody who comes over the embankment on foot. I'm going to go block the exit ramp. I have additional troopers arriving. We don't know what we've got, so we take them only if we have no other choice. If they try to leave, then we do whatever we need to do to prevent that. No hostages, no high-speed pursuit if we can help it. If nothing else, we need to keep them on foot, keep our advantage."

I drove over and pulled car 662 across the exit ramp. Our

current odds weren't great: two killers with a sniper rifle versus four troopers, spread out, with sidearms, but it was going to have to do until I got some more troopers and deputies in place. Help was on its way, but I didn't know when they would get here. This was a familiar situation to troopers assigned to the more rural areas of Maryland. If it took twenty minutes for backup to arrive, that was pretty good. I just hoped we had twenty minutes.

Once I was situated on the exit ramp, it was time for me to take command—time to initiate the incident command structure as I had been trained to do. I ordered a Code 3 on the Frederick Barrack radio channel. A Code 3 meant that all radio traffic was restricted to my command. Unless you had radio traffic specific to this incident, then the order was simple: stay the hell off the radio unless communication was directed at your unit. This also required that all repeater units get turned off except for the unit in the trunk of car 662. Car 662 was now the incident command car.

Word was getting out, at least within law enforcement. The radio, which had remained quiet, was starting to come alive with units from all over the state switching to the Frederick channel and advising their location and the fact that they were on their way. I wasn't sure if there was anything going out over the civilian radio and news channels. But I figured the news channels had picked up on the radio traffic centering on the rest area, since they had known about everything else concerning this investigation, often before the cops did.

"Car 662, be advised," the radio crackled. "Frederick County sheriff's department has a K-9 unit minutes away."

"Ten-four," I said, then turned my attention to the K-9 team. "Frederick County, be advised, when you arrive, cover as much of the westbound median as you can. Frederick, make sure that any units coming my direction run silent with no lights."

"Ten-four, car 662." I then heard the police communication operator put out a general broadcast.

"At the direction of 662, all units responding secure lights and sirens. Six-six-two wants silent response. All cars acknowledge."

This clearly established to all responding troopers and deputies that car 662 was the command vehicle and I had taken command of the situation. There was absolutely no sense in having some overanxious responding trooper or deputy blow what I had hoped was our tactical advantage of surprise by rolling in with siren blaring and lights flashing.

The goal was to have all the K-9 units I had available protecting the quarter-mile distance between the entrance ramp into the rest area and my location at the exit ramp.

I heard a Frederick County sheriff's deputy arrive, and I assigned him to assist me in covering the exit ramp. Sergeant Hundertmark also advised me that he had orders for me to call the task force immediately.

I knew that all the brass housed in the operations center were aware of the sighting and were beside themselves because they weren't on the scene. I could only imagine the conversations and arguments that were going on there. They had to be driving the barrack duty officer nuts with all kinds of demands and requests that he was, from a logistical standpoint, unable to provide. I was also guessing that there were a number of them jumping into cars and heading out like firemen leaving the station for a five-alarm fire.

"I'll contact them as soon as I can," I told Hundertmark, "but I need more time to set and secure a good perimeter. Frankly, it's more important for me to speak with the two witnesses in the rest area. I have one cell phone; the JOC is going to have to wait."

Knowing Sergeant Hundertmark the way I did, he was probably

smiling. "Here's the cell phone of our witness," he said, and he read out the number.

32

It did occur to me that if the press were listening they would now have my witness's phone number. I wouldn't have put it past any of them to try to call the witness directly, which would have cut us out of the communication link and caused a very serious problem. There are certain things that you cannot control in every situation, and the best you can do is try to at least *manage* those things. This was one of those situations: I needed the phone number, so this was a risk I had to take.

I told Hundertmark to keep monitoring the cell phone call. "Relay whatever information you think the JOC needs to know. Oh, and let them know what I'm doing. And tell them we didn't just become troopers yesterday; we know what the hell we're doing."

I got on the cell phone with my two witnesses. I remained calm, mostly for their sake, but also because I wanted to keep my wits about me. I told them who I was and asked them a series of questions. "Do you feel safe? If not, we can sneak a couple of troopers in to get you out."

They told me that they felt safe for the moment. They still were not seeing any movement in or around the parked Caprice, nor anywhere in the rest area.

"Okay, good. Now either a Frederick duty officer or I will remain on the line with you for the duration. If at any time you feel threatened, then we can be there in less than one minute."

I filled them in on my plan, which was to completely surround the rest area with troopers. We would carefully plan the arrest and execute it, I told them, when it was the right time. "This is going to take a considerable amount of time before we're ready, and success is going to depend on your ability to be our eyes. But again, if you feel threatened at any point, just say the word, and we'll get you out."

They were okay with everything I had said. They told their story: The one caller said he was the night caretaker of the rest area. When he pulled into the rest area, he had parked a few spaces from the Caprice. He had been listening to his radio when he heard the description and tag number of the car that we were looking for. He said, "I don't know much about how to read," so he got out of the car and wrote the tag number down on his hand, including the state, with a pen. He didn't have a cell phone or any money for the pay phone, so he found the other person, Mr. Donovan, and asked him to call the police. The entire time, he saw no one in or around the car.

While I was talking to the witnesses, the barrack kept calling me, but of course I couldn't answer even if I had wanted to, since I was on the line with our witness. I understood the frustration of the brass back at the JOC. It's difficult to be forty-five miles from the action and still feel responsible for the result. But it was also obvious to me that these leaders had either never been in the field in the middle of an incident or had forgotten what it was like to be up to your ass in alligators while someone is asking how many alligators you're dealing with. They couldn't help me solve a damned thing over the phone, so they needed to trust me and my training to make the call as I saw fit. And they needed to provide me the resources to get the job done.

Unfortunately, it wasn't that simple. The FBI, the ATF, and all the other agencies had leadership at the table. They didn't understand the state police's culture and training—the culture and training that I represented—and I didn't understand theirs. All these agencies had worked extremely well together over the past three weeks, but it was impossible to blend together all of our differences in such a short time, and under the pressure and stress that this case had created. The straight incident command structure works great when it's one agency. Yet there's always a human factor based upon the different agencies' training and philosophy, and that can throw a monkey wrench into the mix. You can plan for it, you can talk about it, and you can even practice it, given the time and money, but you never know how it will hold up until the proverbial shit hits the fan.

While I was juggling talking with our people in the rest area, listening and responding to the police radio, and maintaining my post, another state police car pulled into the exit ramp and took up a position beside car 662. Again, a lucky break. Trooper First Class Dwayne Smith, at the time working out of the Hagerstown Barrack as a road trooper, was another senior guy and a good man to have around. I had served with Dwayne many times over the years. We had never really worked in the same unit, but he was another former narcotics trooper, who had received the same training I had. We had served search-and-seizure warrants together many times. He was another trooper who wouldn't flinch in the face of a shoot/don't-shoot situation.

Without saying a word, Dwayne handed me his cell phone so I could now talk to the witnesses, talk to the troopers over the radio, and call the JOC all at the same time. Dwayne was armed with a Remington 870 shotgun. I told him that no matter what happened, we couldn't let that car get past us and out of the rest area. Dwayne simply nodded. I didn't have to tell him anything else. Good thing, because it was then that we saw headlights heading our way from the rest area.

A slight left-hand curve out of the parking lot prevented anyone in the truck lot from seeing our location, and any vehicle merging onto the exit ramp from the car parking lot wouldn't see us until it rounded the bend. Likewise, we couldn't know for sure if these headlights were coming from the truck lot or the car lot. I put down the cell phone and radio and advised the barrack that we had headlights coming at us and to stand by. Trooper Smith took up position to my left and behind his driver's side quarter panel. He had his high beams on, and his outside spotlight pointed to the front in the sightline of anybody coming at him. Car 662 didn't have a spotlight, so I had the high beams on and was staying behind my engine block as well. We had both cars across the ramp in a V-shape, with the point directed toward the inside of the rest area, toward the oncoming headlights.

As the vehicle approached, we could tell it was a tractor trailer. The sounds of the diesel engine and the driver changing gears made it obvious. In some respects, I was relieved to realize it was a truck coming at us and not the sniper car. But we weren't out of the woods. The snipers could have hijacked the driver and his vehicle. The truck was a lot higher than our police cars. Although we would be able to see the driver, we couldn't be sure if there was anyone else inside that truck.

As the truck rounded the slight bend we heard the engine change as the driver started to idle down. This was another good sign. Our high beams and spotlight would have blinded the driver, and as long as we were behind the headlights there was no way he could see us or know how many of us there were. We were trying to use every tactical trick we had in our book. Then we heard the release of the air brakes. Trooper Smith had his shotgun pointed at the driver. I approached the driver's-side window slowly, my .40-caliber Beretta drawn. The driver rolled down his window. With my five-cell flashlight blinding him and my Beretta pointed right at him, he looked startled and nervous.

"State police," I said.

He stuck both his hands out of the window.

"Are you alone?"

"Yes," he said.

"Have you been contacted by anybody while in the rest area?"

"No. I pulled in here around ten tonight to get some sleep. I went to the restroom, then I came back to my rig and went to sleep. What the hell is going on?"

"Did you see or speak to anyone?"

"No one."

"Would you step out of the truck so we can have a look, please? You're not in any trouble. You just happen to be in the wrong place at the wrong time."

The driver complied readily. Trooper Smith had quietly slipped around to the passenger side of the truck and had opened the passenger side door, quickly checking the interior of the sleeper cab. The cab was empty, as was the sleeper compartment. I performed a quick pat down to make sure the driver didn't have surprises that I needed to be aware of. It's not unusual for truck drivers to be armed. I had no idea who this guy was; he could be a wanted person who happened to be caught in an unexpected situation and thought we were after him.

"Clear," said Dwayne.

The driver was shaken. "What's going on?"

"Sir, I'm sorry for the inconvenience. But the snipers are in the rest area."

"Holy shit," he muttered, wide-eyed.

"And you saw no one moving around when you pulled out of your parking spot?"

"I didn't notice anyone, no."

"Well, you have two options; you can leave and be on your way, or you could help us out."

He looked back at me, confused.

"Would you like to be a good American? If so, just leave your truck where it is and help us block the exit ramp. That's it. Just leave it here, get in your cab, lock the doors, and get into your sleeper. Mind you, it could be a while before we're able to move in."

The driver readily agreed.

"Another thing," I said. "If you hear any CB radio traffic coming from any of the other trucks still in the rest area, ask them to stay where they are and stay locked in their trucks. And in the event of gunfire, keep your head down. Don't be tempted to look out the windows. Just stay in the sleeper."

The driver climbed back up into his cab. He kept the engine running for warmth, but shut all the lights out. Within a few minutes, a second truck approached us from inside the rest area.

Trooper Smith and I once again cleared this truck and had the driver pull up alongside the other parked truck. Now there would be no way, with the woods so close and an embankment on either side of the parked trucks, that the snipers could get out of the rest area by car.

33

I advised the barrack of what we had accomplished. A frustrated duty officer acknowledged my message and again indicated that the JOC was insisting I call immediately. I checked in on the phone with our two witnesses; they were fine, and nothing had changed. Trooper Draskovic now had two additional uniforms with him at the entrance ramp and felt comfortable that they would be able to prevent the snipers from leaving. Maybe it was the adrenaline, but again I told him, needlessly, that he was not to let that car out of the rest area and he could use whatever force he saw fit.

I assessed our position. There were three K-9 teams positioned in the median strip. Both directions of the interstate had now been shut down. Westbound was shut down at the Myersville exit, which was at the bottom of the mountain approximately two miles east of our location. There was a McDonald's just off the Myersville exit ramp that had a large truck parking lot. That lot was being converted to a staging area for arriving police units, including communications vehicles and armored vehicles that were responding to the incident.

My next order to the barrack was to get the eastbound rest area cleared of all vehicles as soon as they had personnel available. As I looked across, I could see that there were several trucks and cars parked over there. There was no traffic moving on the interstate, and I didn't see any reason for anybody to be in that rest area. I wanted to eliminate any danger to the public, as well as to prevent the snipers from having access to another vehicle in the event that they somehow got out of the rest area and past us.

I wasn't happy about the fact that I still had my two witnesses and at least four other truckers in harm's way, caught inside our perimeter. But there wasn't much I could do about that without running the risk of getting into a gunfight in the dark. That would be to the snipers' advantage, so it was something I was going to do my best to avoid. Just let the bad guys sleep and feel comfortable until the cavalry arrived. I knew the TANGO teams would be on their way to the staging area by the McDonald's, if they hadn't arrived already.

As for the truck drivers, I figured if they would stay in their trucks and stay locked in, that would be my best option. If they tried to leave, they would simply back up behind the two stopped trucks we had added to our roadblock. We would then clear the trucks as they came up, and the drivers could either stay locked in their trucks or we could evacuate them out of the rest area to an area behind our police lines.

I was starting to feel more comfortable about our tactical situation. There were now three of us on this end, and more uniformed troopers arriving. I now had at least ten uniforms in place, and we had them surrounded on three sides. The only open side was the woods, and I wasn't really worried about that as an escape route.

No more delaying it—it was time for me to go back to car 662 and call the JOC. I used Dwayne's cell phone, and said as I was dialing, "Do whatever you need to do. I'll handle the communications." I really didn't have to tell him that. He already knew what needed to be done. It was a good feeling to know that I was surrounded by troopers I knew, and whom I considered to be the best of the best. The snipers' luck had just run out. They didn't yet know it, but I sure as hell did.

It was somewhere around 12:45 a.m. when I finally called the joint operations center. I was immediately placed on speakerphone, probably in the same conference room that I had left several hours before. The FBI special agent in charge was on the line, as was the agent in charge for the ATF, plus at least a dozen other voices. They were all talking at once, asking questions at the same time. They were all trying to introduce themselves, an obvious power play. They wanted to make sure I knew who the real bosses were. But this wasn't a cocktail party; introductions weren't necessary. Plus, I didn't care who they were. I just wanted to make sure the leadership was up to speed and to let them know we had this under control.

I had seen this same group of people in action several hours earlier, so none of this surprised me. This conference call reminded me of standing in the chow line at the JOC behind the heads of the leading federal agencies, listening to them argue over what to put on their plates while the working stiffs stood in line behind them waiting to just get something to eat. I had resisted the urge to yell, "Shut up, eat the cream of mushroom soup, and get the hell out of the way."

I stopped trying to talk. In those first few minutes of this multi-conversation I must have been given at least three dozen orders by people who had no idea what my current tactical situation was or what I had already put in place. Once the initial barrage of chatter started to wind down, I briefed them on the situation. I told them about the two witnesses. That set off rumblings of concern and started up the second-guessing. I assured them that if things went south for the witnesses, I had the resources to take whatever action was needed to get them out of there. Probably none of these people had ever been at this rest area and had no idea of the terrain I was dealing with. I understood their concern, I understood their need to be in control and call all the shots. It was also obvious that they were trying to call the plays and micromanage the incident from forty-five miles away. They didn't know me, which most likely contributed to their anxiety. They had forgotten about the incident command structure that had been ingrained in all of us. They either couldn't trust my training and experience or couldn't let go of their desire to be in charge, probably part of the reason they each had risen in command within their own agencies. I was betting on the latter.

The JOC did reassure me that the TANGO teams would be taking the lead with the assault of the Caprice. I knew Major Ballard would be leading those teams. Having worked with the major, I also knew what he was expecting from my side—hold the perimeter. I assured them that we had the perimeter surrounded, and I explained why I wasn't concerned about their escaping through the woods and across the mountain. I suggested that patrol cars be dispatched to the back-mountain roads closest to the rest area and told to stand by.

We talked about the snipers. I mentioned I thought they were likely sleeping in the car, but I could not be sure one wasn't standing guard, maybe in the woods nearby, while the other one slept. Yet we had no indication of that—no one had been seen moving around in the rest area. I also told them that I was planning for the worst-case scenario, a shootout with the snipers. It's always better to prepare for the worst than just assume these guys would surrender without a fight. They had shot and killed so many people and had a god complex; there was no reason to think they would give up without a fight. I was preparing for that fight, and I knew that Major Ballard was also more than ready to give these scumbags all the fight they wanted. Still, it was extremely difficult to communicate what I knew over the phone to people who were only half listening and probably didn't trust me anyway.

I also told them I believed the element of surprise was on our side and there was plenty of time for the TANGO teams to plan their assault. I explained that the time would also be to our advantage. By the time it was 3 a.m. to 5 a.m., the snipers would be at their most vulnerable and would likely be at their lowest level of alertness. Since I had worked with Major Ballard and the STATE teams so many times before over the past twenty years, I knew he was thinking the same thing. I didn't really need to talk to the major and exchange ideas. I already knew and anticipated what he was thinking. From his perspective, I had all the bases covered.

Yet there was still a big push from the FBI and ATF. They wanted their people in that rest area and in charge. Here we went again: it was professional competitiveness between agencies, and I didn't have time for that bullshit. I had killers locked in a trap, and I was damned if I was going to let the troopers and deputies under my command get hurt over politics. As they pushed harder, I stood my ground. "I know the rest area, I know the troopers I have under my command, I already have communication and have established trust with the witnesses," I said. "There is nothing I need from any of you other than resources when and where I direct them."

But I kept hearing advice and orders issued to me. "Don't do anything until we get there and take command," someone said.

I kept repeating myself: "Got it covered, I know what the hell I'm doing, I'll keep you posted if anything changes, don't worry—I won't let them out of the rest area." I had to work to keep my cool, though what I wanted to do was reach through the damn phone and slap all of them on the backs of their heads. I was dealing with what was in front of me, and making decisions based on a myriad of factors that none of these potentates could possibly know about. I'm sure they all knew that what I was telling them was the right thing. But their anxiety and frustration at not being here were driving them crazy, and their egos were at a boiling point. I understood and respected that. But by the tone of my voice I had let them know I was in charge, and that they were just going to have to trust my judgment.

If there was anything positive about this exchange, it was the fact that all this vitriol wasn't being spewed out over the radio, and none of my troops were hearing it. The last thing that any of them—any of *us*—needed was a distraction. I wanted everyone focused on the job at hand. These were seasoned cops who understood that there can be only one chain of command in an incident like this. I trusted them without exception, and I knew that every one of them had complete trust and faith in me. That's just the way it was—the way it has *always* been throughout the history of the state police. I could have been anybody else sporting a state police badge and it would have been the same.

Out of the corner of my eye I caught a shadow moving up behind me. It was a cold night, and the first thing that registered was that this person was wearing shorts and was carrying some sort of assault rifle. I was still on the phone and stopped mid-sentence: *Fuck*, I thought, *the bastard got behind me and I am dead.* I spun around and reached for my holstered Beretta. The guy was wearing a backward baseball cap and a black tactical vest over a short-sleeve shirt. As he passed under the streetlight, I could see in small white lettering above his right breast area—DEA. There was a badge hanging off the left breast pocket that I believe was sewn on. "Stop!" I shouted.

Trooper Smith and the deputy spun around. Smith leveled his Remington on the guy's chest. The guy shouted "DEA!"

As he got closer I snapped at him. "What in the hell are you doing? Who the fuck are you?"

He told me he had heard about what was going on when he got a call from his supervisor. So he jumped out of bed, threw on a pair of shorts and a T-shirt, and hustled up here. The guy obviously wasn't local; he had been flown in from another part of the country to help on the task force. He said he was planning to sneak into the rest area with his rifle and see what he could see.

It took a few seconds for me to compose myself and not jump down the guy's throat. "Look, I am not your boss, but this is my incident, and I am currently the incident commander until properly relieved. If you go in there and one of my perimeter troopers sees you, you are going to get your ass shot off. My people have been instructed to assume anybody not in uniform is one of the snipers. This is just like a combat zone. Their instructions are to do what they need to do. And here you are, wearing shorts and a T-shirt and carrying an assault rifle. If you think my troops are going to see that two-inch DEA lettering over your pocket, then you're an idiot. And if you go in there and screw up the TANGO team operation, well, if they don't kill you, I might."

The last I saw of the DEA agent was his back as he hurried away.

34

It was a small incident in hindsight, but small incidents can quickly become high-level incidents during events like this. The DEA agent's gaffe drove home the point—this thing still had the potential to spin out of control at any second. It was my responsibility to prevent that from happening. If I didn't maintain command, and if the well-established incident command structure failed, we could have dead troopers, dead civilians, or both. So back to the phones I went, partly because I wanted to verify that we still had a status quo, but also because I needed to settle my nerves and get refocused. I couldn't let what had just happened alter the plan.

I checked in with my witnesses and got their update: nothing had changed. Then I returned to the conference call. "Be advised," I told the egos at the JOC, "I have enough coverage here at the scene. Do not send any more backup until I request it. And I do *not* want anyone near this incident who isn't in uniform. A DEA agent in a pair of shorts carrying a rifle damn near got his fucking head blown off." The response was silence.

I remembered the shooting in Virginia where three hundred cops converged on the crime scene. I didn't want that. There were plenty of people here with guns already, and I wanted to make sure we limited gunfire to the bare necessity. Once that bullet leaves that barrel, there's no calling it back. Plus, I was pretty sure all hell would break loose on the first shot. The situation could go from contained and dangerous to out of control and deadly with one inadvertent pull of a trigger from a nervous cop.

I'm not sure which one of the agents at the other end of the phone said it, but it was said: "This is not a strictly state police operation. My agents will go to that scene."

I'd had enough. Memories of that drug raid gone afoul came pouring back into my mind. Bullets flying and nobody knows who the bad guys are and who the good guys are. The only difference was, this was going to be worse. "No," I said. "This is in the woods. It's dark. We have the perimeter covered. If cops are up here—and I don't care if they're agents, troopers, deputies, officers, or the guy delivering pizza—if they cannot be clearly identified as being in uniform, there's a real risk they could be shot. If they aren't in uniform, I don't want them on the mountain. And if they're already on the mountain, call them back immediately. I've ordered my troopers blocking both ends of the interstate to stop anyone not in uniform unless it's approved by me. I don't give a rat's ass *whose* agent they are, if they're not in uniform then get them the fuck off my crime scene."

There were grumblings from the other end of the phone. The conversation was getting heated. Blood was up, and emotions were edging out common sense. They were ignoring the command structure, focusing instead on which agency would claim the glory when these killers were apprehended.

I'm sure they wanted this case to be over—we all did. And those guys at the JOC had to be under tremendous pressure. It wasn't every case where they had to report back to the White House. I understood. And yet they were back at the JOC, and I was on the scene. I knew my troopers, and I knew the turf. I just couldn't seem to get that through their heads. I was determined to follow our command structure protocol. As long as I was in charge of the scene, that's how it was going to be. I wasn't going to let any cops get sent home in a body bag—not even the dumb ones running around here in the dark in plainclothes and carrying assault rifles.

Another voice came on the line. "This is U.S. Deputy Marshal Johnny Hughes. Lieutenant Reichenbaugh is correct; he doesn't need anyone not in uniform on that mountain. He knows what he's doing. By my authority, he is in charge and is calling the shots up there until the TANGO teams are ready to deploy and execute the arrest." It was a welcome voice from my past. Johnny Hughes, retired major from the Maryland State Police, had moved over to the Marshal's Service after retirement. It was obvious that everyone on the line accepted that he and the Marshal's Service trumped whatever authority they had.

I never did understand all the politics that get involved in cases like this, but the U.S. marshal has the final word, so the problem was quickly resolved. Now I could concentrate on communicating with my two witnesses, who were still very much in harm's way. I could focus on maintaining the perimeter and evaluating any changes that might occur, and what change in tactics that would require. I did not see another plainclothes police officer or agent on the mountain until the whole thing was over.

My senses had been on high alert ever since the initial call from

Sergeant Hundertmark saying the snipers had been spotted in the rest area. My eye was catching any movement, including rustling of the leaves from the slight breeze. I don't know if it was a slight shadow I suddenly saw, a slight and sudden downdraft, or a sensation that I *felt*. But I looked up and saw nothing more than a shadow and a silhouette of a helicopter rotor and the body of some sort of helicopter. The aircraft made no sound and was completely blacked out—no lights visible. It was just a black silhouette against a dark sky.

At first I thought I was seeing things, but I wasn't. The aircraft was up there. It moved low overhead and wasn't far above tree level. I don't know whose aircraft it was, but it wasn't one of the twelve Maryland State Police helicopters. MSP helicopters make a very distinctive whiny sound and would have been heard by everybody, including the sleeping or, for that matter, the dead. This unidentified aircraft was moving very slowly, silently, almost in a hover.

I had a feeling it was being used as an airborne observation post, and that they were using forward-looking infrared, or FLIR, to see if they could pick up any heat signatures coming out of that Caprice—or, more important, an unexpected heat signature in the woods behind the Caprice. It was the smart thing to do, and I had thought about requesting a helicopter to come and take a look for me earlier, but I had nixed the idea because I was afraid the helicopter noise would wake our sleeping killers. To this day I don't know whose helicopter that was. The FBI helicopter I had observed early in the investigation sitting at the Montgomery County police training facility wasn't capable of silence like this craft. My guess was that it was military.

To me, the benefit of calling in one of our choppers earlier was outweighed by the risk at the time. The state police helicopter would have been no different from a news helicopter—noisy. This one was like nothing I had ever seen. There wasn't a sound except the slight rustle of leaves in the tree canopy. Whoever those guys were, I hoped they were wearing white hats and were on my side. Because if it wasn't one of ours, then I had bitten off a lot more than any of us could chew.

But the snipers *couldn't* have access to that kind of technology. It had to be TANGO. That meant the TANGO teams were getting close to deploying and were trying to gather as much intelligence about their target as possible. It wouldn't make any sense to conduct this flyover, then wait an hour. A lot of things can change in an hour in a situation like this. I looked at my watch: It was just after 3 a.m. Most of the area was asleep at this hour. It was time.

My guess was that Major Ballard was in that aircraft so he could get a personal feel for the situation, the layout, the tree cover, and the exact location of the parked Caprice that we believed and hoped the killers were sleeping in. It was still unknown if the snipers were in that car or what they were doing. We still had to assume that one of them could be in the woods with that rifle while the other one slept. But we had seen no changing of the guard in the hours we had been there. As for my witnesses, I was confident that they were wide awake and would have reported any movement. I know this because I was in constant communication with them and asked them about every ten minutes if anything was different.

Less than fifteen minutes later, the Code 3 radio silence was broken. Major Ballard's voice came over the air. "Be advised, TANGO is in route and three minutes out."

"Ten-four, TANGO, I copy," I replied. "Car 662 to all units. TANGO is incoming. Maintain your positions and stay sharp until further advised. Do not react to anything you see or hear coming from inside the perimeter. Maintain weapons discipline and do not fire unless there is a threat directly in front of you that you must deal with. All units acknowledge."

I didn't really need to say what I said, because I knew all the troopers up there on the scene understood how STATE, now incorporated into TANGO, operated. I made the announcement in case there were other agents and deputies that I didn't know about up there hiding in the bushes someplace; if so, I wanted them to clearly understand the orders and know what was expected.

The moment of truth was at hand. If the snipers were in that car, they were about to have justice administered to them. Their reign of terror was over. It was going to be completely up to them if they left that rest area in handcuffs or in body bags. But what if they *weren't* in that car? We would be back to square one. We knew who they were, but we would have no idea where they were, or how they were moving around. Had they carjacked somebody in the rest area? When daylight came would we find the body of another citizen in a ditch or in the woods? Darker yet, was this a trap? Had they lured us in so they could take out a bunch of cops in a last blaze of glory? We could turn from hunters to hunted in one hell of a hurry.

Questions, questions: within a few minutes, we were about to know the answers to all those questions rolling around in my head.

35

TANGO had deployed on foot. They were coming through the woods using night-vision goggles. This was the kind of operation they did well and had practiced over and over within the past three weeks. This team consisted of a full six STATE team members supplemented by three FBI SWAT members and one from the Montgomery County SWAT team. While we waited for TANGO to get in place, I got on the phone again with our two witnesses.

"We're moving in on the Caprice in a few minutes. You may hear a loud noise. If it doesn't go as planned and the suspects aren't sleeping, you may hear gunfire. Don't worry—our teams know where you are. Just stay in your vehicle, and you'll be safe. And no matter what you hear or see, do not get out of your vehicle for any reason. If you feel threatened or if you feel in danger, just start your car and head toward the exit."

I could hear the nervousness in the voice on the other end of the line. "Yes sir, I understand. We have not seen anybody or anything moving in or around that car. Do you think they are still in that car? We won't move or get out."

I talked to them in the most soothing voice I could muster. "Good. Don't worry; we have you covered. I will make sure that nothing happens to you. I can get to your car in under a minute if I need to. Just remember—no matter what you hear, stay in the car and stay low. Stay on the line with me." I remembered the lesson I had learned years ago: Always stay in control, or make it *seem* like you're in control, no matter what the hell is going on.

All the troopers and deputies on the perimeter had heard the radio message from Major Ballard. I didn't need to repeat orders; every one of those troopers had worked with STATE teams before. They wouldn't approach until the scene was cleared by STATE. I could hear and feel the tension in the silence over the radio. Every trooper, deputy, officer, and agent was at a peak level of readiness. It wouldn't take much to set off this powder keg.

I had told the witnesses that I was shrinking the perimeter in their direction in case there was a need to come to their defense.

Trooper Smith, the deputy, and I began our approach on foot from the exit side of the rest area. We spread out in a skirmish line, maintaining a sight line with each other. That gave us better visuals and made each of us a more difficult target in the event the snipers were in fact awake, out of the car, and waiting for us. Our radios were turned down to nothing more than a whisper. The last thing we needed was radio traffic giving away our position.

The night had become still, the breeze had quieted, and the temperature had dropped into the high thirties or low forties. Eerily, the rest area and surrounding woods were extremely quiet. I knew then what it meant to experience deafening silence. Our weapons at the ready, we slowly moved toward our witnesses' vehicle. We were also now able to put ourselves between the snipers and the four or five other sleeping truck drivers who were unaware of what was happening. We were slightly out in the open in the parking lot, but given the surroundings, there wasn't much we could do about that. If the snipers had relocated to one of those trucks now behind us, then our asses were in trouble and we had walked into an ambush that we likely wouldn't walk away from.

I looked across the parking lot in the direction of the parked blue Caprice. I could just see it through the trees, across the lawn and beyond the picnic tables, about 150 yards away. I had the earpiece attached to my portable radio with the ear bud in my right ear. I heard the soft squelch of the radio. Ballard's voice came on briefly. "Thirty seconds out."

I halted our three-man skirmish line. I could only just make out the TANGO teams emerging from the woods behind the Caprice. They were nothing more than dark shadows. They moved quietly and quickly in tactical formation, closing the gap between the parked Caprice and the thirty yards of lawn that separated the parking lot from the tree line. The three of us took cover behind anything we could find. We also got low in the event bullets started flying. TANGO knew we were there. They knew I had shrunk the perimeter on our side to provide cover for our witnesses. Bullets wouldn't come in our direction unless they came from the snipers. TANGO was the best there is on the civilian side of this business.

It was pucker time, that moment when you try to turn your five-foot, ten-inch frame into a three-foot bundle and stuff your entire body behind a tree that was three inches wide.

The TANGO team approached the car and split into two groups, one moving to the driver's side and the other to the passenger side. I knew what would happen next, but my heart still jumped a beat when the teams smashed the two car windows simultaneously. I closed my eyes as I had been trained to do when I heard or anticipated the flash-bang grenades going off. The flash-bangs are just as the term implies. They go off with one hell of a bang and a flash of bright light. The bang is designed to invoke confusion and the flash is to instill blindness because it would happen faster than the killer's minds could process the information or understand what the hell just happened. The few seconds of confusion were all that TANGO would need. I closed my eyes so I wouldn't lose my night vision.

However, what I had anticipated never happened. TANGO had caught them so much by surprise that there was no need to use flash-bangs.

It seemed to be happening in slow motion. I saw hands reach inside the vehicle and bodies being pulled out, one on each side. From where I stood, the snipers looked like rag dolls, one pulled from the front seat and the other from the back seat, then quickly vaulted clear of the car and thrown to the pavement. Two large, heavily armored troopers, complete with Kevlar helmets and their night-vision equipment flipped up and out of the way, leaped on top of them. The troopers worked fast, quickly securing the suspects' hands behind their backs and searching them for weapons.

The radio crackled. Ballard's voice came over the air: "Be advised, the suspects are secured. The scene is secure."

I took a deep breath for the first time in hours. All that anticipation of things going badly wrong, all that thinking and anticipating what the next move would be depending on what happened—it left me in an instant. It was as if someone had finally rolled that dump truck loaded with ten tons of gravel off my chest.

It also felt like victory. We had somehow been able to surround two of the most notorious and cold-blooded killers in American history and end their killing spree without having to fire a shot.

Smith, the deputy, and I made our way through the picnic area to the Caprice and the two suspects, who had been flipped up to sit on their asses Indian style. Two extremely large and well-armed troopers were standing over them, guns trained right at them. I still had two cell phones with me, and both lines were still active. I grabbed the JOC phone and relayed Major Ballard's message.

It may just have been my own tension being released, but I swear I could feel the collective sigh of relief coming through that phone line.

36

Just a few seconds after Ballard declared the scene secure, three or four state police cars came screaming into the rest area, screeching brakes and sliding tires in front of the Caprice, blocking my view of the two killers as I approached. Trooper Draskovic stepped out of one of the cars, and Corporal Poffenberger and his k-9 partner got out of the other.

The joint operations center was asking me to confirm the identities. Time to switch from incident commander to crime scene commander. I didn't want excited and overzealous troopers, agents, deputies, and cops screwing this thing up by being too aggressive. Apparently Major Ballard had also thought about this as well. As I came closer, Ballard was ordering everybody away from the car, and he had formed a perimeter. We couldn't take any risk with the integrity of whatever evidence was in that car. One little mistake could cause an issue at a suppression hearing, which could result in some or all of the evidence getting thrown out of court; in that case these two suspects could walk.

A large roll of yellow police tape appeared out of the trunk of one of the cop cars. "I want at least thirty yards cleared around that car with nobody inside of the perimeter," I ordered.

More law enforcement officers, including Captain McAndrew, my major—Tom Bowers—and Captain Bernie Forsyth, the lead investigator from Montgomery County Police Department, were pulling into the lot.

I walked up to the two suspects and, for the first time, looked into their faces. I immediately recognized both of them from photos: John Muhammad and Lee Malvo. I grabbed the cell phone and reported to the command staff back at the joc: "We have positive identification on both suspects, identified as John Muhammad and Lee Malvo. The suspects are secured."

I hung up. I'd had enough of talking to those guys for one night. Plus, I had to shift gears from hunter and incident commander to criminal investigator charged with making sure this was handled in a professional way. It wasn't just excited cops I had to worry about; I also had to watch the brass who, because of their rank or position, felt the need to just walk up to the car and touch something.

I began taking stock of the surroundings as more and more cops came flooding into the rest area. As I looked again into the face of Muhammad less than ten feet away from me, I saw a man in fear. The fear was in his eyes. He was defeated and looked like he was expecting to die at any moment. One of the TANGO team guys was standing over him, with another less than a step away.

I walked over to where Malvo sat. Drak towered over the kid, and a state police German shepherd stood snarling just inches from his face. I was staring into the face of a killer. Malvo glared back at me. There was no fear in his face. He wasn't intimidated at all, by any of us. I had little doubt that, given the chance, he would have tried to kill every one of us. But guess what? I wasn't intimidated by this little puke. "Trooper Draskovik," I said, "if this shithead so much as farts, snap his fucking neck."

"Yes, sir, no problem at all," Drak said. He had a grin on his face from ear to ear.

Quickly, decisions were made to get these two the hell out of there to a more secure location. The suspects were to be taken back to Montgomery County and directly to Seven Locks, the county jail in Rockville, not far from the JOC and Montgomery County Police headquarters. A police car would lead the procession, occupied by a trooper and two TANGO team members. That would be followed by another cruiser with one of the suspects in the middle of the back seat, with a TANGO team member on either side of him. One of the Montgomery County homicide investigators would ride shotgun. Following that car would be one of our K-9 cars, which would be followed by another cruiser with the other suspect stuffed in the back just like the first one. That car would be followed by another K-9 unit, followed by another trail car containing the driver and two more of the TANGO team members. The bastards would be what we used to call "cuffed and stuffed."

They would be driven down the interstate highway with lights and sirens, not slowing or stopping for anyone, and not permitting any other vehicle to interfere with the motorcade. There would be a state police helicopter "Trooper 3" providing air support for the motorcade.

We expected that word had gotten out. There was no way the media wasn't aware that the snipers had been captured, so we prepped for the potential of news helicopters waiting just outside the no-fly zone, and for news trucks, reporters, and photojournalists hoping to snap a picture of the suspects. We expected them to be stationed all along the interstate and trying to get close.

Muhammad was the first to be moved. He had to be helped to his feet and was obviously very weak-kneed. He was led to the back door of the waiting car. When Malvo was told to stand, he just glared. "I won't tell you again, asshole," said Drak, reaching down with one hand and grabbing him by the back of his shirt and neck and picking him up off the curb. He was then shoved into the back of Drak's car like a sack of potatoes, but never said one word. Within a minute the cars were arranged in proper order, and off they went. My cruiser had been moved, and the truckers were permitted to leave. The rest area had been cleared.

Major Bowers, Captain McAndrew, and Captain Forsyth huddled to decide what would happen next. Forsyth put his arm around my shoulder and, with a big smile on his face, said, "Thank God it was you up here and not one of the agents from out of town, or this would have likely turned into a real cluster."

"No problem, Captain," I said. "Just another day at the office." That was the first smile I had seen on Forsyth's face in three weeks—since before the killing spree began.

Now that the suspects had been removed and there were no longer any exigent circumstances, the team decided it was time for a search-and-seizure warrant. And it would be by the book— we would wait until it was prepared and signed by a judge prior to *any* search of the car. None of us wanted to be the one who made the mistake that allowed these guys to walk. As the saying goes, "Don't be the guy. Don't be the guy to screw up in fifteen seconds all the collective work of a thousand cops. Don't be the guy who caused an entire case to go down the toilet and let killers walk."

We didn't know where the sniper rifle was, if it was in the car or, possibly, hidden somewhere in the woods. We felt good that we had the right car and the right suspects, but we really needed that rifle. McAndrew and I stayed behind and made sure the crime scene was secured. Forsyth and Bowers headed toward Montgomery County to make sure the prisoners were being properly tucked into the county jail, that a plan to interview them was worked out, and that everything was done correctly.

The sun had begun to come up. On the horizon was the promise of a crisp, clear, beautiful fall day in Western Maryland. This would be the first day in more than three weeks that the public could finally relax and feel safe. They were waking up to the news streaming out of this little rest area. The nightmare was over.

The roadblocks had been lifted, and I could hear traffic moving both westward and eastward along I-70. This early in the morning, a growing stream of traffic would be heading east toward Washington and Baltimore. Any delays caused by the drama would surely be forgiven by a relieved public. No more hiding behind fender wells just to put gasoline in their cars. No more running to and from store entrances. No more shades drawn or fear of going outside.

The rest area was now full of federal agents, a few troopers who had been stationed to maintain the police line, and Montgomery County detectives and brass arriving from all the agencies. Not knowing what was going to be needed, I put in a request to have the recruit class going through basic state police training in Pikesville bused over. We would need a grid search conducted of the entire rest area, including the woods, in the event the suspects had left something behind. The class arrived in an hour.

The early morning chill made me shiver, and I decided to walk back to the end of the exit ramp and move my car closer. Both ends of the rest area were still blocked off, now by state highway trucks with arrow boards instead of police cruisers. The state police command bus had been moved into the rest area, providing a warm place to rest and get a cup of coffee. I started in that direction, then decided to visit the men's room first.

Outside the restroom, a man was standing there leaning on some big trash cans on wheels. In the rush of the arrest, I had forgotten about the two witnesses. We had been able to locate the killers, secure the area, and make the arrest without ever having to fire a shot, and none of it would have happened without those two people. This one was the rest area custodian.

"How you doing?" I said. "You okay?"

He was the one whose call brought all of us here. He was also a mentally challenged person.

He looked up and asked, "Lieutenant, did I do a good thing?"

"You have no idea what a great thing you did. As far as I'm concerned, you are a real Maryland hero. You spotted the snipers, then found the other guy and had him make the call."

His expression turned serious, and he was upset. "I don't know anything about being a hero, but I'm worried about my job. I didn't get around to emptying all of the trash cans like I'm supposed to do."

I put my arm around him. "I don't think it's going to be a problem. It was our fault for keeping everyone out of the area, so there probably isn't going to be much trash in the cans. Besides, I'll make sure I clear it with your boss."

He looked at me and thought about it for a second, then nodded and pushed his big rolling cans out toward the truck lot to check on the trash out that way. I have no idea if he realized how important a role he had played in stopping two cold-blooded killers. If he did, he wasn't overly impressed with himself; he was just someone doing what he thought was the right thing to do.

I finally made it out to where I had left car 662. From there I could look out across the interstate to the eastbound rest area—there must have been at least twenty satellite news trucks set up in the parking lot on that side. I don't know what they expected to see from that location, because this rest area wasn't even in their sight line, much less the parked Caprice. But at least they weren't over here trying to get in the way. Still, they had their jobs to do. As much as it pained me to think about it, the media had played a role in helping us communicate with the snipers. They were invested in this outcome too.

37

October 24, 9:30 a.m. About six hours after the suspects had been removed from the Caprice, detectives from Montgomery County, along with their evidence techs and the ATF, arrived in the rest area with the signed search-and-seizure warrant. They got busy sorting their equipment and gloving up so as not to contaminate any evidence.

It was then that I finally had the chance to really look at the Caprice. It was an older model, dark blue with faded paint. It really wasn't a lot different from my unmarked cruiser, except that this one was modified for violence and evil. The doors were still open, just as the TANGO teams had left them. The interior was covered in trash, including fast food wrappers and cups; these two had been living out of the car. As I circled it, I noticed that what was left of the windows had been darkened with cheap window film. I also noticed what appeared to be a small hole cut out of the trim area just above the license plate and below the trunk lid. There was something stuffed in the hole. No rifle was visible inside the car.

We were hoping to find one in the car, and we suspected it would be in the trunk. We knew we had the right guys. Still, there was considerable apprehension waiting to see what was in that car. One tech, armed with a 35-mm camera, was taking what would end up being hundreds of pictures of the area, including where the car was parked and the surroundings. He then focused on the car itself, taking photo after photo of the exterior and what could be seen of the interior from outside. These pictures would eventually be used as evidence in the upcoming trials.

Once the techs had photographed everything, it was time to enter the car. A more detailed forensic examination would later be made when the Caprice was removed and taken to an indoor facility and out of the weather, but we had to make an initial examination while it was at the scene. I was standing by the driver's side door with Captain McAndrew, another detective, and a couple of cops. We were nothing more than spectators at this point. The tech made a cursory scan of the front seat and the back seat, removing and bagging several items, including a laptop.

Then the evidence tech pulled down the back seat, revealing a clear pass-through to the trunk. Behind the back seat in a recessed area, there it was—a Bushmaster .223-caliber assault rifle.

It was a surreal moment, staring at the very weapon that, presumably, had been used for all the shootings. After three weeks of intense investigation and searching, I couldn't help feeling taken aback by how the rifle just popped into view when the back seat was pulled down. So easily, in direct contrast to how hard we had worked to find it.

Multiple pictures were taken before the weapon was touched by the evidence tech. As he took the rifle from the car, he pulled back the receiver to make sure there were no rounds in the chamber. One round came tumbling out.

I was mesmerized. The small brass shell spun in the air and landed on the pavement, making a tinkling sound as it hit and rolled under the car. Whose name would have been on that bullet? Had we not reached these guys in time, who might have died?

It is amazing how events we are not even aware of can change our life forever. Somewhere out there, someone is obliviously alive today because we caught these guys before they could shoot again. As it turned out, this was the only bullet the snipers had left. Had we not stopped them, they would have used it, no question. Then the only thing stopping them would have been lack of ammunition. Could they have gotten more? Stores in three states had pulled their .223 ammo off the shelves, at least until this was over. So the snipers were, quite literally, down to their last bullet.

Over the next hour or so, the evidence guys went over the car, collecting various items and evidence that would later be used successfully in the trials of Muhammad and Malvo. As I watched the techs uncover more evidence in the car, it became clear that this Caprice had been a mobile office, so to speak, for the shooters. The back seat gave them access to both the hidden rifle and the car's trunk, without their ever having to get out of the car. The windows had been tinted to make it impossible for the casual observer to peer inside. The small circular hole cut just under the trunk lid allowed a shooter lying in the trunk to put the muzzle of the rifle through the hole without being seen. When the hole wasn't in use, they filled it with an old glove.

Maybe for extra camouflage, the snipers had spray-painted the underside of the trunk lid blue. When they opened it slightly, it would have blended in with the rest of the car. When they were in shooting position, the trunk lid would have been open; the shooter, lying in a prone position, could control how wide it was open using a piece of electrical wire hooked to the latch. This ensured enough space for the rifle's EOTech holographic weapon sight to fit through the trunk opening. Unlike the stock or iron sights that would have come standard with the rife, this higher-end sight featured an optic sighting system that allowed the shooter to fire accurately in low lighting situations. The rifle had been fitted to kill. The trunk needed to be open just two inches to give the sight line the snipers needed. The sound or report of the fired rifle would have been absorbed by the trunk and interior of the Caprice. Once the shot had been taken, the shooter would pull the trunk lid shut, withdraw the rifle barrel, shove the glove in the hole, and the driver could leave the area quickly and quietly without ever stepping outside the car. Cover, concealment, and mobility—the car had been carefully planned out and prepared.

Plus, the old car was ordinary. There was nothing special about it that would stick out or cause anybody to really take notice, and it easily blended into traffic. A lot of thought had gone into turning this run-of-the-mill car into a snipers' nest for cold-blooded killers. Every detail was considered, right down to spray painting the inside of the trunk lid blue so anyone who happened to look in their direction wouldn't notice that the trunk was slightly open. This also explained why they were reluctant to abandon this car for something else during their three-week killing spree.

They planned each kill, and they killed based upon their plan. This wasn't about a desperate man seeking revenge against an ex-wife over child custody, as had been portrayed. Maybe that was what set Muhammad off, but this much planning and premeditation suggested terrorism—the *desire* to kill.

When the evidence guys finished their initial search, the car was loaded onto a car hauler and taken to a police lab in Montgomery County, where it could be more carefully searched for forensic evidence. Taking no chances, we removed the car under heavy police escort, with an officer riding with the hauler operator, and several police cars in front and behind, including me in car 662 bringing up the rear.

We were escorted back to Montgomery County by news helicopters filming the entire entourage, as well as news trucks with photographers hanging out the windows trying to get pictures of the Caprice. As the adrenaline was wearing off, I felt heavy exhaustion beginning to take hold. I had forgotten how tired I had been when this whole thing started—fifteen hours ago. I had been thirty hours without sleep, and now that we were in the wrap-up stage, it was catching up with me. But there was still work to do.

We headed east on Interstate 70 and made the southward turn onto Interstate 270 toward Montgomery County. Since I was heading back to the joint operations center, I broke off from the motorcade. As I passed the car hauler, I took one last look at the sniper car that had eluded us for the past three weeks.

At the JOC, I gave a quick debrief to both the command staff and my intelligence group and partners, those people I had spent the past three weeks working with. There were smiles, hand-shakes, and slaps on the back. I was relieved, but I didn't feel all that happy. I couldn't stop thinking about the victims and their families—fourteen people who had been shot, ten of whom had been killed. Yes, catching the snipers was a victory in the sense that they would never kill again. But it never should have gotten that far in the first place.

I addressed the group. "Every member of this group and every member of this task force deserves as much, if not more, credit than I do. Each and every one of you was part of a team, and it took the entire team to solve this, to track these killers down. I just happened to be a guy trying to get home who wound up being the incident commander. But it's all of you who helped make this happen."

An hour later, after I had been thoroughly debriefed, Captain McAndrew sought me out. "We need to go over to the ATF lab," he said. "They're getting ready to test fire the Bushmaster. And I'll drive. You look like shit."

"And I probably look a whole lot better than I feel," I said.

At the lab, we were escorted to an area that contained several firearms examiners. Lying on a table was the snipers' rifle. A chill went down my spine; here was the gun that had killed ten and seriously injured four more. One of the lab guys explained all the nomenclature of the weapon. We stepped away from the table and into a room where we could watch through a glass window as the rifle was loaded and fired into a block of gel-like material. That would allow the team to capture the bullet so it could be examined and matched to bullets recovered from the victims. Even though I knew the weapon was going to be fired, and even though we were separated from the lab and had ear protection, the report of the rifle still made me jump. The last time it had been fired, a bus driver had lost his life.

I had been around firearms all my life, starting at around seven years old when my dad taught me how to shoot a little .22-caliber Crickett rifle. I have never seen anything inherently evil about guns. They were nothing more than tools to be used for hunting, target shooting, and gun sporting events such as trap shooting and skeet. For me, guns had accounted for hundreds of hours of good times hunting with my dad, my grandfather, and my brother. It had never crossed my mind to use a firearm against a human being. When I became a trooper, my firearm was a tool, just like a hammer is to a carpenter. No gun is evil unless it's used in the hands of an evil human being. The same can be said about a knife or an auto that is being driven by a drunk driver.

But the report of that .223-caliber Bushmaster assault rifle as it was being test fired was chilling to me.

The bullet was removed from the gel. It took less than fifteen minutes for the expert to make a preliminary match of that bullet to others that were in evidence from the killings. There was no doubt this was the rifle that had been used by the snipers to shoot these people.

We left the lab and went back to the JOC. I walked straight to car 662 and headed home for the first time in days. I'm not sure how I made it there, I was that exhausted. I pulled up in front of the house, then picked up the radio and called Frederick Barrack.

"Frederick, this is car 662. I'm 10–42." Out of service. Home.

———

October 24, 4:42 p.m. The sun was beginning to set. In the house, Jean was waiting for me. My teenage daughter came bounding down the steps. "Dad, did you hear? They caught the snipers! We'll have our game tomorrow night! Will you be there to watch me cheer?"

It was time for me to put the Beretta back in the gun safe, hang that state police Stetson on a hook by the coatrack, and turn from Lieutenant Reichenbaugh, Maryland State Police, operations commander, Criminal Intelligence Division, to just the most important title there is—Dad. I looked into those blue eyes and couldn't help but think about those ten people who no longer could do what I was doing. I smiled at my daughter. "I wouldn't miss it for the world."

EPILOGUE

In the days and weeks following the capture of the Beltway snipers, the joint operations center and the SNIPMUR Task Force were officially wound down, as the team of more than one thousand agents, troopers, deputies, and officers returned to their normal assignments. The investigation would continue for several more months, however, as investigative teams traced the snipers' movements and pieced together information, evidence, and intelligence in an attempt to determine what exactly these killers were responsible for, and also to understand what made them tick.

I don't think any of us who worked on that task force for those twenty-three days will ever forget that case and the pressures we were all under, from the citizens we serve to the governments we work for. Every case takes its toll and a small chunk of our armor, but state troopers have been answering that call in Maryland since 1921 and will continue to do so far into the future. On my last business card before I retired was a saying that I believe to the bottom of my heart: "Maryland State Police, a solid tradition protecting lives and property."

Follow-up investigation revealed that the afternoon before they were captured, Muhammad and Malvo had been spotted picking up cans in the woods across from Myersville Elementary School. The witnesses who saw them and their parked car thought they seemed suspicious, but didn't think enough about it to call police.

I believe the snipers' last bullet was meant for a child at Myersville Elementary School, a final "screw you, cops" before the killers moved on to parts unknown. These two were smart enough to know they were never going to get money from the government, so they needed to get out of the area, commit a few more robberies, and buy more ammunition. This wasn't about money, and I seriously doubt they truly believed in the grandiose plan that Malvo confessed to. This was about killing. They got off on it, and they very much enjoyed the publicity they generated for themselves.

After months of investigation it was determined that they were connected to and responsible for seventeen killings and the wounding of ten other people in Alabama, California, Florida, Georgia, Louisiana, Texas, and Washington State. That doesn't include their shootings in Maryland, Virginia, and the District of Columbia. Because of the wide geographic scope of their crimes, there was some political wrangling over where the snipers should be tried. Prosecutors everywhere they had been felt pressure to claim a piece of their asses and make them answer for their crimes.

Ultimately, they were tried first in Virginia. In September 2003, a Virginia court found Muhammad guilty of the murders committed in Virginia and sentenced him to death. In October, Malvo was tried as an adult and was given six consecutive life sentences without the possibility of parole; Virginia couldn't go after the death penalty because Malvo was seventeen when the murders occurred. Both Muhammad and Malvo were also tried in Maryland in 2006 and were also found guilty of their crimes.

On November 10, 2009, the state of Virginia executed John Allen Muhammad by lethal injection at the Greenville Correctional Center in Jarratt. Lee Boyd Malvo remains incarcerated in Virginia.

ACKNOWLEDGMENTS

Those twenty-three days in October became part of the most massive and intense criminal investigation and manhunt in American history. On the heels of the terrorist attacks of 9/11 and the uncertainty of the anthrax case (which at that time had not been solved), our nation was on edge. We all feared that sooner or later our country would come under attack again. To many people, the snipers running unchecked around Maryland, Virginia, and D.C., and killing at will, brought terror once again into American living rooms.

For law enforcement, this case became the ultimate test of our ability to maintain that thin blue line and keep people safe. Local, city, county, state, and federal agencies came together, setting aside egos (for the most part) to form a single focus and track down the snipers. This book was written to preserve the details of this extraordinary case.

I want to acknowledge the victims and their families who were devastated by the sniper attacks. Neither their tragic losses nor the losses of their families will ever be forgotten.

This book is also dedicated to the thousand or so police officers, detectives, deputies, troopers, civilian police employees, and agents who worked this case—none was more important than any other. They unselfishly set aside their lives and poured their hearts and souls into tracking down the killers and bringing them to justice.

I want to thank the National Law Enforcement Museum, which

will soon open a new, first-of-its-kind facility on E Street NW in Washington, D.C. The museum curators permitted me extraordinary access to the case files, crime photos, and the physical evidence I needed in order to complete this book. The evidence from the Beltway sniper case, as well as from other infamous cases, will soon be on display to help track the history of law enforcement in this country.

For those who would like to better understand the lessons that law enforcement learned from the sniper investigation, you can go online to the Department of Justice website and review the white paper *Managing a Multijurisdictional Case: Identifying the Lessons Learned from the Sniper Investigation,* by Gerard R. Murphy and Chuck Wexler, with Heather J. Davies and Martha Plotkin. I used this document to assist me in re-creating the timeline.

I would also like to thank my collaborator, Lori Widmer, for her assistance in the writing of this story, and for the encouragement she provided. I couldn't have done this without her. Lori gave me the best advice she could have ever given when, after several months of outlines and kicking around ideas, she said, "Dave, just write the story and stop sweating the details."

I would also like to thank my kids for the sacrifices they made during my entire career, sacrifices shared by the families of every law enforcement officer: missed ball games, missed birthday parties and Christmas mornings, and for some, the dad or mom not coming home at the end of the shift. To those who paid the ultimate price to stand as part of the thin blue line, you are forever in our hearts and on our minds; you will never be forgotten.

Lastly to Jean. It takes a special kind of person to be married to a cop and put up with the job and the stresses. For more than thirty years, Jean has been there on those bad days to console me and dry my tears because of some of the things I've seen or had to do. She has also been there for the good days and the successes I have had, and has always welcomed those successes with the biggest smile. Most important, she has kept the family together. Without her, I'm not sure where my career would have taken me. I always made a point to kiss her as I was heading out the door for my next shift. Without saying a word, we both understood there was a possibility I wouldn't come home. That took a special woman and a special kind of dedication and love. Thank you, Jean, for the sacrifices you have made to support your trooper.

INDEX

Note: Page references followed by a *p* indicate
a photo between the pages listed.

52–54, 63, 67–68, 79, 194; intuition, 87–88; physical demands on, 94–95, 124–25, 191; traffic stops, 23–25, 33–34; transfer requests, 16–17. *See also* Maryland State Police (MSP)

U.S. Marshals Service, 49, 50, 74

van (white): database search for, 56, 65, 80; media reporting, 36, 69; police lookouts, 33, 83, 133, 134; tips on, 11, 29, 36–37, 45, 69, 82, 85–86, 91, 97, 119

vehicles: helicopters, 104, 145, 175–76, 184, 191; license plate checks, 88–90, 114, 116, 119–20; Maryland State Police, 10, 33, 142, 148–49; roadblocks, 91–92, 93, 104, 166, 167, 185; secrecy about, 133; tips received on, 29, 40, 45, 68–69, 82, 83, 85, 143; tractor trailers as barricades, 150–51*p*, 163–65; traffic stop precautions, 131, 133. *See also* Caprice; van

victims. *See* shooting victims

Virginia: Ashland, 103, 106, 108, 150–51*p*; community standstill in, 2; Falls Church, 96–98; Fredericksburg, 45–46, 70–71*p*, 91; Manassas, 70–71*p*, 83

Virginia State Police, 46, 49, 83

Walekar, Premkumar, 28, 70–71*p*

Ward, Vonzell, 14

Washington, D.C.: community standstill in, 2; D.C. Metropolitan Police, 41, 43, 95; shooting in, 39–40, 41

Washington State, suspects linked to, 113

weapons. *See* ballistics

Wheaton, Maryland, shooting in, 9, 27, 70–71*p*

Williams, John Allen. *See* Muhammad, John Allen

witness accounts, 26–27, 29, 40, 45, 68–69, 97, 117. *See also* tips and leads